Profit by Investing in
Real Estate Tax Liens

Second Edition

Also by Larry Loftis:

Successful Real Estate Investing in a Boom or Bust Market

Investing in Duplexes, Triplexes, & Quads:
The Fastest and Safest Way to Real Estate Wealth

Profit by Investing in
Real Estate Tax Liens

Second Edition

Earn Safe, Secured, and Fixed Returns Every Time

Larry B. Loftis, Esq.

KAPLAN

PUBLISHING

New York

Vice President and Publisher: Maureen McMahon
Acquisitions Editor: Michael Sprague
Senior Managing Editor: Jennifer Farthing
Production Editor: Fred Urfer
Development Editor: Joshua Martino

Published by Kaplan Publishing,
a division of Kaplan, Inc.

Printed in the United States of America

November 2007

07 08 09 10 9 8 7 6 5 4 3 2 1

ISBN 13: 978-1-4277-9595-3

Kaplan Publishing books are available at special quantity discounts to use for sales promotions, employee premiums, or educational purposes. Please email our Special Sales Department to order or for more information at, kaplanpublishing@kaplan.com, or write to Kaplan Publishing, 1 Liberty Plaza, 24th floor, New York, NY 10006.

DEDICATION

This book is dedicated to Gemma Dela Rosa, without whose help, support, and encouragement this book would never have been written.

Contents

PART ONE
INVESTING IN TAX LIENS

PART TWO
INVESTING IN TAX DEEDS

PART THREE
LIST OF STATES

My greatest debt of gratitude is to Gemma Dela Rosa, who worked tirelessly on the first edition of this book, and again researched all 50 states to make sure our information in Part III was correct and up to date for this second edition. She has been with me at the vast majority of tax sales where I've bid or invested, has spoken with county officials in almost all 50 states, and has invested in numerous states herself. She is a tax lien expert in her own right. In short, this book would not exist without her and my thanks to her will never be adequate.

I would like to thank my first editor, Mary B. Good, for believing in the original project and being the nicest person to work with in the publishing industry. I also would like to thank Shannon Berning and the entire team at Kaplan for suggesting a second edition and bringing it to fruition.

When my publisher approached me about writing a second edition of this book, I was pleased to do so for two reasons. First, I wanted to delete many of the photos in the book (and all with me in them) and explain why they were in the book in the first place. When I wrote the first edition, I had been lecturing around the country on tax lien and deed investing. During this time, I met and heard many who claimed to be experts, but who had purchased no liens or deeds themselves (or very few). I was shocked by the false information being touted in order to sell book and tape programs or expensive seminars. For example, the sales hype I heard often claimed that liens are "guaranteed" by the county or government. That is never the case, as anyone who has been to a single sale would know. A second common pitch is that it is fairly common to get a nice house for pennies on the dollar at a tax deed sale, or on the post redemption side of a lien sale. As one who has purchased liens and deeds in 10 states and been to sales in another 4 states, I can assure you that this is extremely rare. I've never even done it (I once bought a small house in a rural area of Kansas for $4,100, but it needed a ton of work).

So the reason I included photos, including photos of me at auctions, was to show the reader that I actually had firsthand experience. The photos were not for self-aggrandizement (I actually don't like my photos floating around the country, especially when I'm having a bad hair day!), but for credibility. I believe that an author—especially one claiming to be an expert—should have considerable personal experience in what he or she is writing about.

Since the first edition of this book, which was published in November 2004, at least four other books on purchasing tax liens and deeds have been published. Without exception, none of the authors claims to have any experience personally buying tax liens or deeds. One book even touts in its subtitle, "How to Guarantee

Your Return Up to 50%." As anyone who has been to a lien or deed sale knows, the county *never* guarantees anything, and most clearly state in their materials *caveat emptor*—let the buyer beware." I don't know about you, but I don't want to be the patient of the surgeon who has only read about surgery on the Internet! While tax lien and deed investing is not brain surgery, it can be complicated and confusing, especially when states sometimes use legal jargon, different meanings for the same terms, complicated bidding or legal foreclosure proceedings, and so on.

For this edition, I've omitted all of the photos of me at live auctions, but I've retained copies of relevant county material and photos (just smaller, however) of relevant properties. I think it is imperative, for pedagogical reasons, for you to see what the counties actually give you at the auctions.

The second reason I wanted to write a second edition was to give you an update on online bidding and new tax lien laws. While online bidding has spread throughout Florida, it has been slow to catch on in other states. Some states have also enacted new laws regarding tax lien and deed sales (Rhode Island and South Dakota, in particular). So, in Part Three of this edition, I'll update you on new laws and counties that have adopted online bidding, where applicable.

I hope you find this new material useful. I wish you every success in your lien and deed investing.

Larry B. Loftis
March 2007

INVESTING IN TAX LIENS

1

IF THIS IS SO GOOD, WHY HAVEN'T I HEARD ABOUT IT?

If you picked up this book, you likely already have heard about investing in tax lien certificates. If you are like most people, however, you know little about it. For years, stories have circulated in real estate seminar circles about the fabulous benefits of this type of investment. Unfortunately, the speakers touting the benefits often know little about it and exaggerate the benefits in order to sell a product or service. More often than not, these speakers either have never bought liens at all, or have purchased just a handful of small liens in one state. Sometimes, the misinformation comes from a real estate author who writes a very short section on tax liens (or an entire book) to illustrate another way to make money in real estate. In every case I know of, these authors have never personally purchased a lien.

I was listening to a seminar not long ago when I overheard a young man at the back tables (he worked for the company sponsoring the seminar) discussing tax liens with another person. He made several erroneous comments, until finally I could not take it any longer and had to jump in. According to him, you could invest in a lien in Texas and get a guaranteed 25 percent interest rate. In that one sentence, he had made three errors.

First, Texas is a deed state, not a lien state. As such, an investor is buying a deed, not a lien. Second, rates are never "guaranteed." Rates are fixed by statute, but an investor only gets that rate if the owner redeems (i.e., pays off the taxes and penalties). Third, Texas involves a penalty, not an interest rate. With a penalty, one pays the same amount, regardless of when the redemption occurs.

This young man was very confident and matter-of-fact about his knowledge and wanted to impart his expertise to those around him. I knew what had happened. Somewhere, this young man had heard a seminar speaker exaggerate claims about this investment. More than likely, the seminar speaker may himself have just heard this information from another. Like other rumors (what us lawyers call "hearsay"), these stories tend to get bigger as they pass from one person to the next. So I said to him, "Really, have you ever been to a tax sale in Texas?" Knowing the answer, I wanted to see just how far he would go. He stumbled for words for a moment or so and finally admitted that he'd never even been to a Texas sale. "Let me see if I can help you," I said. After spending a few minutes correcting all of his comments about Texas, he finally said to me, "We need to go to lunch."

On several occasions, I've heard seminar speakers state emphatically that a Florida lien pays a guaranteed 18 percent. I will get into specifics of lien investing later in this book, but suffice it to say that the rate is never guaranteed and is seldom 18 percent (Florida is a "bid down" state and bidding starts at 18 percent). Many years ago, it was not uncommon for a Florida investor to get plenty of small liens at 17 to 18 percent (I had plenty in 1999 and 2000). By 2001, people were exiting the stock market and institutional investors were rushing into tax liens and bidding down to 5 to 7 percent. I managed to get a few liens at 18 percent (see Figures 1.1 and 1.2). By 2004, most good liens were being bid down to 0.25 to 5 percent. I was working hard to get 14 to 16 percent. In 2005 and 2006, most good liens were bid down to 0.25 percent (thanks, in part, to online bidding). That's

FIGURE 1.1 *Orange County Certificate of Sale Billing*

CERTIFICATE SALE BILLING

DATE: 06/05/2001

BUYER NO:

BIDDER NO: 302

NAME: LOFTIS COMPANIES INC THE

ADDRESS: 205 E CENTRAL BV STE 500
           ORLANDO FL 32801

TOTAL CERTIFICATES $3,879.38   6

LESS DEPOSIT   1,000.00

BALANCE DUE $2,879.38

PLEASE REMIT BY CASHIER'S CHECK, MONEY ORDER, OR CASH

TO: EARL K. WOOD, Orange County Tax Collector
     P. O. BOX 2551
     ORLANDO, FLORIDA 32802

PAYMENTS NOT RECEIVED IN THIS OFFICE BY JUNE 15, 2001
       WILL RESULT IN FORFEITURE OF DEPOSIT
            AND LOSS OF CERTIFICATES.

FOR FURTHER INFORMATION, PLEASE CALL:

     TINKA DOUGHTY - (407)836-2708

EARL K. WOOD, TAX COLLECTOR
The Sun Trust Center Tower • 200 South Orange Avenue • Reply To: Post Office Box 2551 • Orlando, Florida 32802-2551
(407) 836-2705 • http://www.tax.co.orange.fl.us

FIGURE 1.1 *Orange County Certificate of Sale Billing (Continued)*

```
BYRLST                          EARL K. WOOD
                         ORANGE COUNTY TAX COLLECTOR
                          CERTIFICATE SALE SUMMARY
                   TAX YEAR 2000    SALE DATE  5/25/2001         PAGE    1

BUYER:  302  LOFTIS COMPANIES INC THE


ITEM NO    CERT NO      PARCEL NUMBER          PERCENT          AMOUNT
-------------------------------------------------------------------------
   2413   2001-001748   15-21-28-0000-00056     18.00           177.81

   2623   2001-001923   16-21-28-0000-00148     18.00           114.98

   5359   2001-004069   11-23-28-0319-02140     13.00           354.65

   8780   2001-006690   25-22-29-6677-16060     18.00         1,685.03

  13779   2001-010580   07-22-30-5905-00402     18.00           842.94

  16653   2001-012710   17-22-31-2339-11110     18.00           703.97



           SUB TOTAL CERTIFICATES:        $3,879.38           6
```

not the yield the investor receives (Florida has a minimum 5 percent penalty), but you get the point. The "18 percent guaranteed interest rate" discussed at real estate seminars was laughable. Later in this book, I'll explain how a knowledgeable Florida investor can still earn yields of 8 to 12 percent.

To be sure, the benefits of tax lien investing are phenomenal, especially when compared to other traditional investments like the stock market. Consider the chart in Figure 1.3 comparing a tax lien certificate to a stock market investment.

Let's look further at these benefits and others.

Rate of return. Even in the days of bull stock markets, most investors were very pleased to receive safe returns of 10 to 15 percent. In some years, however, stock investors have been happy just to retain their principal. Tax lien investors can perform

FIGURE 1.2 *Orange County Certificate of Sale Billing*

CERTIFICATE SALE BILLING

DATE: 06/05/2001

BUYER NO:

BIDDER NO: 303

NAME: LOFTIS LARRY

ADDRESS:

TOTAL CERTIFICATES $1,447.04   5

LESS DEPOSIT   1,000.00

BALANCE DUE $447.04

PLEASE REMIT BY CASHIER'S CHECK, MONEY ORDER, OR CASH

TO: EARL K. WOOD, Orange County Tax Collector
     P. O. BOX 2551
     ORLANDO, FLORIDA 32802

PAYMENTS NOT RECEIVED IN THIS OFFICE BY JUNE 15, 2001
     WILL RESULT IN FORFEITURE OF DEPOSIT
         AND LOSS OF CERTIFICATES.

FOR FURTHER INFORMATION, PLEASE CALL:

     TINKA DOUGHTY - (407)836-2708

EARL K. WOOD, TAX COLLECTOR
The Sun Trust Center Tower • 200 South Orange Avenue • Reply To: Post Office Box 2551 • Orlando, Florida 32802-2551
(407) 836-2705 • http://www.tax.co.orange.fl.us

FIGURE 1.2 *Orange County Certificate of Sale Billing (Continued)*

```
BYRLST                        EARL K. WOOD
                        ORANGE COUNTY TAX COLLECTOR
                         CERTIFICATE SALE SUMMARY
                    TAX YEAR 2000    SALE DATE  5/25/2001        PAGE     1

BUYER:  303  LOFTIS LARRY


ITEM NO    CERT NO       PARCEL NUMBER           PERCENT          AMOUNT
--------------------------------------------------------------------------
   2275   2001-001647   11-21-28-7906-01120       18.00           844.41

   2497   2001-001817   15-21-28-1190-00030       18.00           110.90

   2821   2001-002073   22-21-28-0000-00172       18.00           119.72

   2973   2001-002174   25-21-28-9252-06040       18.00           189.46

   4068   2001-003114   13-22-28-0000-00019       18.00           182.55



         SUB TOTAL CERTIFICATES:         $1,447.04          5
```

better. In many jurisdictions, the tax lien investor can get returns of 10 to 25 percent, or more. While it is possible to get lower returns because of an investor's desire to buy more liens (spending millions of dollars), savvy investors also can get higher yields by investing in "penalty" jurisdictions (see Chapter 3). I have found that it is fairly easy to get 10 to 16 percent returns in most lien jurisdictions.

Control. Unlike with almost every other high-yielding investment, investors in tax liens have virtually total control in most areas. For example, investors can choose the type of jurisdiction in which they would like to purchase a lien, the size of the lien they would like to purchase, the type of property they would like as collateral, and the interest rate they would like to receive. What these investors cannot control is the time within which the property tax

FIGURE 1.3 *Comparison of Tax Liens and the Stock Market*

Criteria	Tax Liens	Stock Market
Rate of Return	10% – 25% or more (in the better states)	11% average
Control	Total	None
Security (Collateral)	Yes	No
Time Required	Light to Moderate	Light to Moderate
Liquidity	Low	High
Volatility	None	High
Commissions	None	Yes (and/or trade fees)
Risk	Low	Medium to High

is paid (although it cannot be longer than the statutory redemption period).

Security (collateral).　Not only are investors' investments secured by real estate, they also have a *first position* lien. That is, the lien comes before a mortgage or trust deed (i.e., the bank) and any other liens on the property, other than something like a county's "weed lien" (where the property was abandoned and the county had to mow it for sanitary purposes).

Let me now ask you a question or two about banks. First, why do you think banks often escrow property taxes on a new mortgage? Answer: Because banks know that the property tax lien comes before their mortgage. If the taxes were not paid, the bank would have to pay the taxes to protect its position, or else be wiped out by a tax lien foreclosure. Second, why do you think banks themselves invest in tax liens? Answer: Because banks intimately know the safety of the investment—tax liens have a higher priority or safety than even their mortgages!

Time required.　How long does it take to invest in this type of investment? I listed the time involved as light to moderate. Yes, an investor must spend some time learning how to do this, how his or her county sale works, and must either go to the sale or send a representative. Many counties are now allowing an investor to buy online. Yes, this takes time. A stock market investor also spends some time choosing a broker, selecting stocks or mutual funds, making trades, watching the market trends, and so on. My guess is the time is about the same.

Liquidity.   Like a certificate of deposit, tax lien certificates are illiquid. Investors cannot expect to receive their principal and interest until the full redemption period has expired. This time is normally one to two years. However, if an investor buys 20 liens in a state that has a two-year redemption period, my experience has been that 10 will pay off over the course of the first year, and the remaining 10 will pay off over the course of the second year. Of those paying off in the first year, probably three or four will redeem a month after the sale (a particularly nice thing in a penalty state).

Volatility.   For many people, the tax lien's stability is the most attractive element. Unlike a stock, the tax lien certificate does not fluctuate in value. If you buy a $2,000 lien at 15 percent, that's it; the interest rate is fixed, much like a certificate of deposit. In penalty jurisdictions, you actually have an upside because the "interest" is actually a penalty, which means that your yield will increase if the owner pays off the lien faster.

Commissions.   Unlike the stock market, tax lien investing does not involve brokers; thus, no commissions are incurred.

Risk.   The risk in buying a tax lien or deed is simple: Counties are ruthless in selling liens or deeds on worthless properties. If you know what you are doing, you eliminate this risk. In the stock market, risk also varies according to the quality of the security. Most stock market investors recognize risk and reward differences when buying a penny stock versus shares of IBM.

Administration. Many people are comforted by the fact that this type of investment is administered by the government. As such, the investor need not worry about fraud, insider trading, Ponzi schemes, or such other negatives to other investment vehicles. Having said that, I will tell you that many county tax collectors are ruthless in selling liens on worthless properties. I'll help you steer clear of those potential risks in Chapter 7.

Enforcement. As a lawyer, I was most pleased to learn that this type of investment is obviously legal, because it is set forth in the laws of every state (more on South Carolina later). Second, if an owner does not pay the property taxes, the remedies also are set forth in state law. Third, the statutory remedies almost never require any kind of formal legal action, but usually just involve legal notices and county-assisted procedures.

With excellent rates of return, strong collateral as security, no volatility, and these other benefits, tax liens compare very favorably against the stock market and other traditional investments. With these obvious benefits, how is it that most people know very little about investing in tax lien certificates?

First, this type of investment does not involve brokers. As such, you will not find advertisements in *Fortune, Forbes, Money,* or other financial magazines touting the nice returns or other benefits of tax lien investing. If the big Wall Street firms do not get a broker's fee to sell you this investment, why would they get involved? Having said that, some institutional investors actively invest in these certificates. For example, First Union Bank (now Wachovia) has invested in tax liens for years. So has Bank Atlantic. I've heard that Merrill Lynch has jumped on board as well.

Second, the element of competition works to keep this investment a secret. All tax lien sales are conducted with some sort of auction bidding process, so that the fewer investors at the event, the better returns or more liens one can buy. As such, every new person who arrives at the lien sale (or bids online) is a potential competitor. Since most sales involve literally thousands of liens costing millions of dollars, the "little" investor is no threat to anyone. However, adding one more institutional investor could affect everyone's success, since that one investor may have over a million dollars to invest that day. Consequently, most tax lien investors do not spread the word on this type of investment.

Third, the government is administering the auction and the process. In most cases, the county municipality is in charge, while in a few jurisdictions the city is authorized to sell liens. Do you think the government goes out of its way to advertise this auction? Has the government ever been very good at marketing? Come to think of it, I have never seen a government advertisement to promote its tax sale. Of course, the county will "notice" the sale (typically several times) in the local newspaper, buried in the back section of the paper. Most people don't even receive a local newspaper at home, and those who do simply assume this section of the paper involves legal notices like foreclosures and other such notices required by statute.

Finally, many people who might know just a bit about tax lien sales shy away from them for lack of knowledge. Most real estate investors and real estate brokers I know have heard of tax liens, but none of them really knows how they work. Many potential investors assume that they need a real estate background to buy these liens. Others assume that they might need legal expertise, just as foreclosure investing requires some knowledge of relevant laws. Still others shy away because they assume the investment is too risky. A book agent once told me that this type of investment contains two words that people inherently fear: *tax* and *lien*. Finally, most investors know that some time is involved in understanding the process and going to the actual sale, and they would rather just call their broker to order a stock trade.

For all of these reasons, tax lien investing has remained "under the radar" for the vast majority of investors. Over the past eight years, however, more investors have been willing to learn more about this unique investment. In large part, this interest was created by the disastrous bear market of 2000–2003. Most stock market investors, including many institutional investors, were battered and bloodied during those years, and many found their way into tax liens.

WHAT IS A TAX LIEN?

Every state and county in the United States levies property taxes on real property. Property taxes are also levied in Canada. With the exception of Indian reservations, every property has taxes due on it each year—vacant lots, residential homes, apartments, commercial properties, shopping centers, and skyscrapers. While you may complain about such taxes on your own property, these taxes allow counties to provide necessary services to the local community, services like police protection, fire departments, libraries, schools, and local roads. In short, your community and mine could not operate and function normally without property taxes.

Each year, the local taxing jurisdiction (usually the county) will assess taxes due on each property and send the owner of that property a bill for the taxes due from the prior year. If the owner does not pay his bill by a certain date, the county (or city in some cases) will levy a lien against that property for the amount of the tax bill. In addition, the county will charge interest and costs to the owner (otherwise, no one would pay their taxes on time!). The county, of course, will send several notices to the owner stating that the taxes are due, and that a late payment will incur additional charges.

Can you see the problem for the county? If many people pay their property taxes late, how does the county make its payroll and provide the necessary services like police and fire protection? Here's how—the county will lien the property and then sell the lien to an investor at a tax lien sale. The investor will have a first position lien (or, in some cases, be second only to a prior *property tax lien*), and that lien will accrue interest and/or penalty from the date of the investor's purchase. When the property owner finally pays his property tax bill, he simply pays the county the delinquent taxes, plus the interest and/or penalty, and the county immediately cuts a check to the investor for his initial principal (the tax bill) plus the interest rate or penalty return. In short, everyone wins. The property owner gets additional time to pay his or her tax bill, the county gets the money it needs now to run the local government, and the investor gets a very nice, safe, secured return. Figure 1.4 illustrates the cycle involved. Figure 1.5 shows an actual tax lien I bought in Iowa on the house in Figure 1.4.

FIGURE 1.4 *The Tax Lien Cycle*

GOVERNMENT

24%

OWNER   FMV = 80K   INVESTOR

PROPERTY TAX = $918

FIGURE 1.5 *Iowa Tax Lien Purchase*

```
        CERTIFICATE OF PURCHASE AT TAX SALE NUMBER 01-1772
          TREASURER'S OFFICE, SHELBY COUNTY, STATE OF IOWA

I, KATHY STINN              , TREASURER, DO HEREBY CERTIFY THAT ON THE 18 DAY
OF JUNE,        2001, AT THE REGULAR      TAX SALE PUBLICLY HELD ON THAT DATE,
THE FOLLOWING PROPERTY SITUATED IN SHELBY COUNTY WAS SOLD TO:
LARRY LOFTIS;205 E CENTRAL BLVD;SUITE 500;ORLANDO;FL;32801

FOR THE AMOUNT OF TAXES, INTEREST AND COSTS DUE AND REMAINING UNPAID.

DIST SH-CP                      TAXED TO: NEUMAN, DAVID B
ASSHC  PARCEL 832916000003      & GAIL A, SURV

LEGAL DESCRIPTION:     33-78-40            PT NW SW

YEAR TYPE  RECEIPT    AMOUNT     INTEREST      COSTS       TOTAL
1999 RE   90998.0     838.00      76.00         4.00       918.00
                                 SUBTOTAL                  918.00
                                 CERTIFICATE FEE            10.00
                                 GRAND TOTAL               928.00

**********************************************************************
THIS BID WAS FOR A 100% INTEREST IN THE PROPERTY.
**********************************************************************

WITNESS MY HAND:
DATE JUNE 18, 2001            Kathy Stinn
                             _____
                             TREASURER OF SHELBY COUNTY,

**********************************************************************
ASSIGNMENT:  FOR THE PAYMENT OF $_____, AS PER AGREEMENT, I HEREBY
ASSIGN ALL RIGHTS, TITLE, AND INTEREST IN THIS CERTIFICATE TO:
_____  SS_____
DATE _____
01-1772            _____
                   ASSIGNOR
```

At this point, you're probably wondering how long the property owner has to pay the delinquent taxes and penalty. The time period for this payment is called a "redemption period" and varies by state. While the range varies from six months to four years, most states give the owner one to two years to redeem. This means that the owner could wait until just before expiration of the redemption period and then come in to the county to pay his tax bill and penalty. As such, there is good news and bad news for the investor.

The good news is that the investor does not need to do anything for a year or two (until the owner pays or the redemption period expires) and all the while his or her investment is accruing interest at a very nice fixed rate. For most lien jurisdictions, the statutory rates allow for interest ranging from ¼ percent to 18 percent. A few states allow for rates offering much better yields. More on that later.

The bad news is that his investment is illiquid for a period of time matching the redemption period. For example, the redemption period in Florida is two years. While the owner could pay off that lien in one month, the investor might have to wait up to two years until he or she gets paid. Most lien investors actually like having their investment accruing at a good rate for as long as possible. For example, if you bought a lien at 15 percent, you would like for it to stay outstanding for as long as possible.

At this point you probably are thinking, *What if the owner does not pay off his or her tax bill by the end of the redemption period?* Just like any other secured investment, the lien holder will move to foreclose on the lien. Recall that the lien holder is in first position, even ahead of a bank's mortgage on the property. In some cases, the lien holder will force a public sale of the property and get paid the principal plus penalty and costs. In other cases, the owner will get the property, free and clear of all other liens. This subject matter will be discussed thoroughly in Chapter 6.

You also may be wondering if this occurs in all states. The answer is "yes" and "no." Yes, all states have some process for enforcing payment of property taxes. About one-half of the states are tax "lien" states, while the other half are considered tax "deed" states. Thus far, the process I've described is the tax lien process. In a deed state, the county is not selling a lien on the property for failure to pay property taxes; rather, the county is actually auctioning the property itself to pay the taxes. Part Two of this book will analyze the process of tax deed sales.

All states will fall into one of three categories:

1. Lien states
2. Deed states
3. "Hybrid" states

A "hybrid" state is technically a deed state. However, it operates like and has much in common with a lien state. In other words, it has aspects of both systems. Let's review the aspects of each.

Lien state:

- The investor has only a *lien* on the property and does not have any other rights in, or title to, the property.
- The investor receives a statutory interest rate until the property tax is received.
- The property owner has a statutory redemption period within which he or she must pay the tax bill.

Deed state:

- The investor actually acquires title to the property.
- No interest rate or redemption period is involved since the investor received the property itself.

Hybrid state:

- The investor actually acquires title to the property, subject, however, to the prior owner's right to redeem and get the property back.
- Should the prior owner redeem (i.e., pay the tax bill plus interest, penalties, and costs), the investor will receive an interest rate or penalty payment on his or her investment.
- The prior owner has a specified redemption period (six months to three years) to redeem the property and re-acquire title.

Figure 1.6 will classify each state into one of these three categories.

LARRY'S REMINDERS

- Tax lien rates are fixed, but not guaranteed.
- Property tax liens are *first* position liens, even ahead of a bank's mortgage.

FIGURE 1.6 *State-by-State Listing of Lien, Deed, and Hybrid States*

Lien	Deed	Hybrid
Alabama	Alaska	Connecticut
Arizona	Arkansas	Delaware
Colorado	California	Georgia
District of Columbia	Idaho	Hawaii
Florida	Kansas	Louisiana
Illinois	Maine	Massachusetts
Indiana	Michigan	Pennsylvania[1]
Iowa	Minnesota	Rhode Island
Kentucky	Nevada	Tennessee
Maryland	New Hampshire	Texas
Mississippi	New Mexico	
Missouri	New York[2]	
Montana	North Carolina	
Nebraska	Ohio[3]	
New Jersey	Oregon	
North Dakota	Pennsylvania[1]	
Ohio[3]	Utah	
Oklahoma	Virginia	
South Carolina	Washington	
South Dakota[4]	Wisconsin	
Vermont		
West Virginia		
Wyoming		

[1]Pennsylvania counties may operate under the hybrid system where the property is improved and has been legally occupied 90 days prior to the sale.
[2]New York City also is allowed to conduct tax lien sales.
[3]Ohio is historically a deed state; however, counties with populations over 200,000 also are allowed to conduct lien sales.
[4]As of July 1, 2006, South Dakota counties may no longer sell tax liens.

- The *redemption period* is the time during which a property owner must pay off his or her property tax lien. This period ranges from six months to four years.
- A tax lien is only a lien against a property, while a tax deed (acquired through a deed sale) conveys title to the property.
- About one-half of the states are lien states and half are deed states. A few deed states are hybrids, because they operate like lien states.

2

THESE LIENS MUST BE ONLY ON CRACK HOUSES, RIGHT?

One of the funniest things I hear when I discuss tax liens with others is the misconception that these liens are only on very bad properties, "crack" houses, for instance. The thinking goes like this: If the owner cannot pay the tax bill on a property, usually only 1 to 2 percent of the property's value, then the owner must be in real trouble and it must be a lousy property. Nothing could be further from the truth. Granted, out of several thousand liens outstanding, certainly some will include vacant lots and small houses in bad areas. Be-fore continuing, let's just analyze that. So what if the collateral is a small lot (as long as it has some value) or small house in a bad area? Taxes still represent 1 to 2 percent of the value of the property. Isn't the risk the same as if it were a very large house, since the 1 to 2 percent tax bill will still apply?

But let's put this all in perspective. Tax liens occur on all types of properties—big houses, small houses, million-dollar homes, condominiums, apartments, shopping centers, commercial buildings, even skyscrapers. I have seen liens on Walt Disney World, McDonalds, Atlantic Gulf Oil, BellSouth Mobility, Amoco, and dozens of other prestigious corporations. See Figure 2.1. I heard that some years ago the Sears Tower in Chicago had a tax lien on it. In my hometown, Orlando, one of the city's landmark properties, Church Street Station, had a tax lien on it. Actually, the property is a complex of buildings, and so there were several liens on the entire complex. See Figure 2.2. At the 2004 sale I bought liens on four properties in this complex (they all paid off quickly). In the late 1970s, this entertainment complex was the number two attraction in Florida, behind

FIGURE 2.1 *Corporate Tax Lien Examples*

ID	Parcel	Code	Name	Amount
	Vizcaya Townhomes			
5891	34 23 28 8883 00030	(U)	Applied Building Devl Of Orl B H Inc	269.28
5892	34 23 28 8883 00040	(U)	Applied Building Devl Of Orl B H Inc	269.28
5893	35 23 28 0000 00060	(U)	Mcdonalds Corp	
			One Mcdonalds Plaza	11,059.82
Hollywood Plaza				
5894	36 23 28 3787 00050	(U)	Sita Resorts Inc	129,553.04
Plaza Intl Ut 11				
5895	36 23 28 7165 00018	(U)	Orlando Convention Partners L P	231,835.62
Plaza Intl Ut 3				
5896	01 24 28 7154 01060	(U)	Ansari Tahir & Ansari Jasmine	19,598.92
Plaza Intl Ut 5				
5897	01 24 28 7158 01000	(U)	Plaza International Restaurant Inc	76,939.26
5898	02 24 28 0000 00003	(U)	Central Florida Investments Inc	18.51
5899	02 24 28 0000 00009	(U)	Maali Enterprises Inc	
			C/O Park Inc	20,784.06
6926	26 24 28 0000 00036	(U)	Shabel Arleen J & Shabel Jack &	421.49
Mckoy Land Co Sub				
6927	26 24 28 5357 00491	(U)	Friedman Sam L & Friedman Rita J	217.25
Lake Bryan Ests				
6928	27 24 28 4336 00110	(U)	Ansari Tahir & Ansari Jasmine	31,712.25
Lake Bryan Shores				
6929	27 24 28 4340 00010	(U)	Water Sports Management Inc	8,976.37
6930	28 24 28 0000 00030	(U)	Walt Disney World Hospitality &	
			Recreation Corp	88,156.47
6931	34 24 28 0000 00010	(U)	So Yee Kwong &	
			Cheng Janey Chu Fang	5,160.05
6932	34 24 28 0000 00026	(U)	Gonzales Andres	8,226.26
Munger Willis R Land Co				
6933	34 24 28 5844 00660	(U)	Buena Vista Hospitality Development	
			Partners Lc	25.55
10860	02 23 29 6808 04010	(A)	Carolstan Properties Ltd Lllp	1,583.98
10861	02 23 29 6808 04011	(A)	Carolstan Properties Ltd Lllp	3,974.65
Poinsettia Park				
10862	02 23 29 7192 0421	(A)	Atlantic Gulf Oil Co	6,615.87
Westwood Gardens Sub				
10863	02 23 29 9232 00020	(A)	Major Willie Mae	HX 403.34
10864	02 23 29 9232 00050	(A)	Infinity Group International Inc	1,231.84
10865	02 23 29 9232 00130	(A)	Dewitt Clairnel N	HX 193.56
10866	02 23 29 9232 00300	(A)	Inlet Properties Inc	1,141.35
Westwood Gardens 1st Add				
10867	02 23 29 9234 02140	(A)	Horton Chris & Horton Joanne	926.12
10868	02 23 29 9234 02150	(A)	Hill Jimmie Royal Jr	HX 224.42
Work Release Ctr Rep				

FIGURE 2.1 *Corporate Tax Lien Examples (Continued)*

14856	25 22 30 8937 00040	(U) Rodriguez David & Alicea Ileana	HX 1,214.87
14857	25 22 30 8937 00210	(U) Llera Dora Alamo	HX 1,365.95
14858	26 22 30 0000 00008	(U) Rotenberger David M Jr &	
		Rotenberger Barbara	13,471.86
14859	26 22 30 0000 00018	(U) Valencia College Shopping Center Ltd	17,626.46
14860	26 22 30 0000 00026	(U) Tischler George W &	
		Tischler Leslie A	2,055.68
14861	26 22 30 0000 00031	(U) Grimsby Orchards Properties Inc	4,686.51
14862	26 22 30 0000 00054	(U) Judd Mary G 1/14 Int &	396.89
14863	26 22 30 0000 00060	(U) Amoco Oil Co	3,360.37
14864	26 22 30 0000 00066	(U) Dade Savings & Loan Association	938.31
14865	26 22 30 0000 00073	(U) Metro Paving & Development Inc	1,359.19
14866	26 22 30 0000 00074	(U) Wiggins Theodore B &	
11373	35 22 29 3772 02030	(A) Miller Theresa	1,482.52
11374	35 22 29 3772 02060	(A) Paul Rinette C/O Arlene Paul	711.48
11375	35 22 29 3772 02080	(A) Laurent Ivertina & Emile Kelly	1,263.51
11376	35 22 29 3772 02150	(A) Hill Robert J Jr & Hill Gladys	HX 565.91
11377	35 22 29 3772 03020	(A) Bell Robert A & Bell Mary S	1,054.13
11378	35 22 29 3772 03051	(A) Anderson Howard	173.49
11379	35 22 29 3772 03060	(A) Hunt Suzie	1,451.29
11380	35 22 29 3772 03070	(A) Hunt Suzie	1,348.85
11381	35 22 29 3772 03140	(A) Brown Michael	2,697.71
11382	35 22 29 3772 03160	(A) Brown Michael	2,486.86
Lamb T A Sub			
11383	35 22 29 4956 00010	(A) Bellsouth Mobility Inc	13,763.63
Long L B 1st Add			
11384	35 22 29 5200 00100	(A) Trabulsy Solomon & Trabulsy Sy E	3,002.99
Lucerne Oaks Condo			
11385	35 22 29 5273 02190	(A) Foster Patrick	761.83
Lucerne Park			
11386	35 22 29 5276 03200	(A) Citiwide Distributions Inc	378.63
11387	35 22 29 5276 04230	(A) Mending Hearts Charities Inc	80.36
11388	35 22 29 5276 09080	(A) Lester Daisy Mae Life Estate	

Walt Disney World. I've also seen tax liens on virtually every major bank, including Chase Manhattan Bank, LaSalle National Bank, Wells Fargo, Bank of New York, Citibank, Bank One, SunTrust, Bank of America, AmSouth, and First Union (I bought liens on Chase and LaSalle). See Figure 2.3. And let's not forget the government itself. I have seen liens on cities (like the city of Hollywood, Florida), the U.S. Post Office, and even the United States of America! See Figure 2.4 for these examples.

FIGURE 2.2 *Church Street Station, Orlando, Florida*

A few years back, I bought a lien on a commercial property (see Figure 2.5) that was originally a medical office building. When I went to take a photo of the building, I noticed about 16 sheriff's cars in the parking lot. I also noticed several reserved

FIGURE 2.3 *Bank Lien Examples*

19852	22 22 32 0712 16710	(U)	Monroy Herbert	352.51
19853	22 22 32 0712 17006	(U)	Francisco Douglas C	352.51
19854	22 22 32 0712 17011	(U)	Morton Thomas S	427.63
19855	22 22 32 0712 17035	(U)	Perez Evangelina	255.05
19856	22 22 32 0712 17090	(U)	Jablonsky Tracy L	134.02
19857	22 22 32 0712 17290	(U)	Senay Marie A	197.07
19858	22 22 32 0712 17550	(U)	Duke Eula & Oser Barbara J	528.04
19859	22 22 32 0712 17590	(U)	Morton Thomas S	544.29
19860	22 22 32 0712 17680	(U)	Lasalle National Bank Tr C/O Superior Bank	1,196.55
19861	22 22 32 0712 17730	(U)	Carrogan Properties Inc	73.51
19862	22 22 32 0712 18100	(U)	Bailes Leman & Bailes Nancy	255.05
19863	22 22 32 0712 18260	(U)	Clark Debra	224.81
18554	16 22 31 8972 00010	(U)	Garrett Wendy E	677.20
18555	17 22 31 0000 00012	(U)	Farias Jaime & Farias Myrna G	2,153.12
18556	17 22 31 0000 00032	(U)	Suntrust Bank Tr C/O Jones	10,269.67
18557	17 22 31 0000 00055	(U)	White Michael A & White Charlotte Ann	1,268.58
18558	17 22 31 0000 00059	(U)	Pidikiti Nanni	5,102.84
18559	17 22 31 0000 00063	(U)	Masswig Gerhard & Masswig Jean A	HX 247.64
18560	17 22 31 0000 00072	(U)	Sanchez Jose G & Rivera Aurea E	HX 671.14
18561	17 22 31 0000 00075	(U)	Rossman Nancy A C/O Prn Investments	5,350.07
18562	17 22 31 0000 00076	(U)	Pidikiti Nanni	171.82
18563	17 22 31 0000 00093	(U)	Sanchez Jose G & Rivera Aurea E	139.84
Arbor Woods Ut 3				
18564	17 22 31 0230 00711	(U)	Pacholski Joseph	1,241.59

			Mitchell Ronald J	HX 723.06	4
Breezewood Ut 3					
4041	12 22 28 0888 01630	(U)	First Professional Investment Group Inc	HX 968.19	4
4042	12 22 28 0888 01730	(U)	Solomon Ronnie & Theogene Renee	HX 1,246.06	4
4043	12 22 28 0888 01960	(U)	Citibank N A Tr C/O Option One Mortgage Corp	1,667.60	R
Breezewood Ut 4					4
4044	12 22 28 0890 02480	(U)	Davy Leonie	1,622.39	R
4045	12 22 28 0890 02490	(U)	Spencer Jack H & Spencer Kathy A	HX 972.86	4
Bretwood					4
4046	12 22 28 0900 00050	(U)	Gillette Eric	2,115.66	R
4047	12 22 28 0900 00130	(U)	Monnestime Gabriel & Monnestime Jeannine L	HX 1,665.92	4

parking spaces marked "Patrol Lieutenant" and "Patrol Commander." Guess who now was the major tenant of the building? The local Sheriff's Department! Can you connect the dots? If the property taxes were not paid, who would be enforcing my lien?

FIGURE 2.3 *Bank Lien Examples (Continued)*

Angebilt Add				
10871	03 23 29 0180 02010	(A)	Gaddy Danny C	1,337.54
10872	03 23 29 0180 02150	(A)	Henry Michael B	1,008.03
10873	03 23 29 0180 03030	(U)	Statewide Capital Inc	801.75
10874	03 23 29 0180 03050	(U)	Federal Home Loan Mortgage Corp	1,526.87
10875	03 23 29 0180 03060	(U)	First Union National Bank Of De C/O Homeq Fidelity	779.29
10876	03 23 29 0180 03101	(U)	Church Orlando Congregational Jehovah Witness Inc	33.77
10877	03 23 29 0180 03150	(U)	Infinity Group International	
2574	27 23 29 8086 06260	(U)	Jean Ernst E & Jean Mona	HX 1,112.72
2575	27 23 29 8086 06350	(U)	Weeks Thomas B Ii & Whitaker David E	HX 1,086.26
outhland Executive Pk				
2576	27 23 29 8194 00001	(U)	Fnb Properties Inc C/O First Union National Bank	23.68
2577	27 23 29 8194 00012	(U)	Amsouth Bank	24,478.02
2578	27 23 29 8194 00020	(U)	Fnb Properties Inc C/O First Union National Bank	45.77
2579	27 23 29 8194 00040	(U)	Fnb Properties Inc C/O First Union National Bank	82.17
lando Central Pk No 24				
2580	28 23 29 6339 02000	(U)	American Metal Investments Inc	14,583.18
lando Central Pk No 34				
13131	22 23 29 2792 04010	(U)	Eberle Richard D	HX 1,399.79
13132	22 23 29 2792 05040	(U)	Harvill Joseph R & Harvill Linda J	HX 2,513.07
13133	22 23 29 2792 07010	(U)	Heron Christopher	543.69
13134	22 23 29 2792 07060	(U)	Pedraza Juan R & Pedraza Diane R	HX 995.95
13135	22 23 29 2792 07220	(U)	Wells Fargo Bank Minnesota N A Tr	HX 1,274.43
13136	22 23 29 2792 08010	(U)	Rodriguez Ismael	HX 2,160.90
13137	22 23 29 2792 08050	(U)	Mercado Emilio & Mercado Adelina	HX 652.17
13138	22 23 29 2792 08062	(U)	Ocasio Hugo & Carrasguillo Norma	HX 651.58
Orange Blossom Park				
13139	22 23 29 6204 01090	(U)	Colman Frankie S 61 1/2% &	419.86
Orange Blossom Terrace				
13140	22 23 29 6208 01120	(U)	Hernandez Milagros	HX 861.23

The Sheriff's Department . . . on their own building! In case you are wondering, yes, the lien paid off in due time.

And don't think the wealthy are exempt from this process. I have purchased liens on million-dollar homes and million-dollar

FIGURE 2.3 *Bank Lien Examples (Continued)*

13145	22 23 29 6208 05160	(U)	Williams Rosemary	1,463.88
13146	22 23 29 6208 06130	(U)	Dandrade Kirth &	
			Dandrade Margarita	HX 762.05
13147	22 23 29 6208 08120	(U)	Atlantis Investment Inc	1,082.32
13148	22 23 29 6208 08140	(U)	Diaz Antonio Jr & Diaz/Mydia	1,331.66
Prosper Colony Blk 1				
13149	22 23 29 7268 07005	(U)	Yeh Eddie & Yeh Vivien	1,371.48
13150	22 23 29 7268 07014	(U)	Holley William I & Ward W T	38.24
13151	22 23 29 7268 08004	(U)	Chase Manhattan Bank Tr	638.91
13152	22 23 29 7268 21001	(U)	D C Holding Co Inc	748.62
13153	22 23 29 7268 21004	(U)	D C Holding Co Inc	3,640.08
13154	22 23 29 7268 22007	(U)	D C Holding Co Inc	2,155.23
13155	22 23 29 7268 23010	(U)	Zimmer Donald R	HX 870.94
13156	22 23 29 7268 24016	(U)	Kelley Kathy L	HX 595.19
13157	22 23 29 7268 25001	(U)	Wheeler Joseph P Jr Tr	1,508.78

commercial properties. I have purchased liens on an NBA Hall of Fame player (Julius "Dr. J" Erving) and a world champion boxer (Hector "Macho" Camacho). See Figure 2.6. I have seen liens on household names such as Wimbledon champion, Steffi Graf, tennis player/model Anna Kornikova, three-time Master's champion, Nick Faldo, NFL football stars Thurman Thomas, Darryl Talley, and Jeff Blake, NBA stars like Dominique Wilkins, Anfernee "Penny" Hardaway, Dennis Scott, Darrell Armstrong, and Rony Seikaly, and major league baseball stars like Juan Gonzalez and Cy Young and World Series winner, Frank Viola. See Figure 2.7. Even celebrities like Wesley Snipes and Carrot Top have had liens on properties. See Figure 2.8. In Figure 2.9, you'll see the Dr. J property on which I bought a lien. Dr. J bought two condos at the top of this nice building and made a penthouse. Since there were originally two properties and two deeds, there were two liens on the property. I bought the first one. Yes, the lien paid off about a month later.

I know what you are asking right now. These people make millions of dollars a year, why aren't they paying their property tax bills? While it is possible that these wealthy individuals did not pay on time because they thought they could invest their money elsewhere and make more than the lien amount in interest, that's

FIGURE 2.4 *Government Lien Examples*

4416	18 22 28 0000 00060	(F)	Kumbry Robert A	765.71
4417	18 22 28 0000 00062	(U)	King Gladys W & Womack Madeline A &	1,156.52
4418	18 22 28 0000 00079	(F)	Bank Of West Orange Attn: Property Dept	12,254.38
4419	18 22 28 0000 00080	(F)	Environmental Landscape Specialists Inc	2,181.11
4420	18 22 28 0000 00081	(F)	United States Of America C/O Property Manager	1,167.76

Grace Park

4421	18 22 28 3116 01010	(F)	Ocoee Holding Co Inc	1,002.46
4422	18 22 28 3116 01020	(F)	Ocoee Holding Co Inc	2,106.76
4423	18 22 28 3116 02070	(F)	Terry Edward J Tr C/O S A Tarr	4,725.06

11216-PT-01300   12151
ORANGEBROOK VILLAS CO-OP UNIT 13,
ABRAHAM,LILLIAN 1/2 INT $609.82

11217-00-00700   12152
17-51-42 SE1/4 LESS SCL RR R/W & LESS PTS SEE
TAX ROLL FOR ADDITIONAL LEGA, CITY OF HOLLY-
WOOD $146,537.64

11217-01-01100 *   12153
MEEKINS HILLS 32-32 B LOT 22 W1/2,23,24 E1/2 BLK
10, SATCHELL,DEVEN & MARIA $3,278.27

11217-02-08200 *   12154
ORANGEBROOK GOLF ESTATES 99-1 B LOT 7 BLK 9

11219-01-05100
CARVER RANCHES 19-2
MAE &

11219-01-05700 *
CARVER RANCHES 19-2
VIOLA

11219-01-06200 *
CARVER RANCHES 1
BROWN,LOUIS B SR LE

11219-01-06310
CARVER RANCHES 19-2
AIR & MITTIE B

9714	26 22 29 6184 00010	(A)	Lutfi Investment Co Inc	6,651.4:
9715	26 22 29 6184 00050	(A)	Burgess Theodore L	660.6'

Orange Grove Park

9716	26 22 29 6236 00060	(A)	Deleveaux Wanda D & Deleveaux Vera J	846.1:
9717	26 22 29 6236 00590	(A)	Lewis Albert Jr	1,017.1{

Not In File

9718	26 22 29 6407 00100	(A)	United States Postal Service	9,916.0

Parramore James B Add To Or

9719	26 22 29 6716 03011	(A)	Barnes George T Jr C/O Virginia Barnes	168.1(
9720	26 22 29 6716 03041	(A)	Peacock J Thomas	4,257.4:

unlikely. First, where could they get those kind of returns with relative safety? Second, they are busy people with little time to be snooping around to make a little bit extra return on their money.

FIGURE 2.5 *Commercial Lien: Medical Office Building*

My guess is that 90 percent of the time these people simply missed the payment deadline. Remember that celebrities and athletes often have little experience in the financial world and often hire someone else to manage their financial affairs. Many of these individuals have a financial company that pays their bills and the financial company may have either missed an invoice or never received it from the athlete/celebrity owner.

In the case of developers or real estate investment companies, many times the developer will hold off on paying the bill until that company finds a buyer for the property (and the tax bill is paid out at closing). Several years ago, the *Orlando Sentinel* ran a story on an upcoming tax sale and interviewed a developer who said he didn't pay his taxes on time because he saw it like a short-term loan, only without bank fees and closing costs.

In 2003, I bought liens on Chase Manhattan Bank and LaSalle National Bank (see Figure 2.3). Why would these national banks own residential properties? This seems easy enough to figure out. Years before, the banks originated or bought a loan on a residential property and the loan went into default. What does a bank do

FIGURE 2.6 *Celebrity Property Liens: Julius Erving and Hector Camacho*

8775	25 22 29 6677 08020 (A)	Halley William J Iii	2,580.69
8776	25 22 29 6677 08060 (A)	Maxwell Bernard & Maxwell Ruth	HX 895.29
8777	25 22 29 6677 13090 (A)	Halley William J Iii & Halley Laura C	HX 1,385.64
8778	25 22 29 6677 15010 (A)	Dong Jeffrey Tr	1,660.88
8779	25 22 29 6677 16040 (A)	Zijl Adolf Everhardus	2,991.35
8780	25 22 29 6677 16060 (A)	Erving Julius W One Magic Pl	1,685.03
8781	25 22 29 6677 16070 (A)	Erving Julius W One Magic Pl	2,991.35
Reeves House			
8782	25 22 29 7340 01040 (A)	Young Sherwin F	HX 1,865.32
8783	25 22 29 7340 05060 (A)	720 Inc	3,752.54

Diamond Cove Ut 2			
6016	10 24 28 2035 01230 (U)	Winker Joseph K & Winker Karen L	HX 3,364.95
6017	10 24 28 2035 01710 (U)	Camacho Hector	4,915.39
6018	10 24 28 2035 01820 (U)	Antonov Stoimen & Antonov Anna	3,500.27
6019	10 24 28 2035 01840 (U)	Florza Lisa Marie	HX 2,066.16
6020	10 24 28 2035 02330 (U)	Pouk Robert	HX 3,808.21
Emerald Forests Ut 1			
6021	10 24 28 2491 00050 (U)	Bottles Mark D & Bottles Tracy L	HX 5,101.78
6022	10 24 28 2491 00120 (U)	Kim Sung Y & Kim Jia S	5,123.18
6023	10 24 28 2491 00450 (U)	Labranche Regina P	5,532.71
Emerald Forests Ut 2			
6024	10 24 28 2495 01740 (U)	Evans Michael B & Evans Donna E	HX 5,146.11
6025	10 24 28 2495 02410 (U)	Valderrama Luis A	4,543.44

when a loan goes into default? Yes, the bank forecloses and gets the property itself, since that was the collateral for the loan. When the bank becomes the new owner of the property, do they also inherit the real estate taxes due? Of course. When the bank takes the property back in a foreclosure, often the bank will not pay the tax bill immediately but will wait until it can resell the property and, like the developers, deduct the property taxes at closing. Don't

FIGURE 2.7 *Sports Star Property Liens*

Keenes Pointe of 2				
5825	29 23 28 4075 03700 (U) Daoud Maher & Daoud Tina			3,716.09
5826	29 23 28 4075 03980 (U) Thomas Thurman L & Thomas Patricia A			35,331.20
5827	29 23 28 4075 04580 (U) Stamper John G & Stamper Leeanne S			5,408.92
5828	29 23 28 4075 04870 (U) Baldez Neves Jose Maria & Baldez Sandra Regina Dos Santos			12,802.15
5829	29 23 28 4075 04890 (U) Christopher Wren Inc			1,388.43
5830	29 23 28 4075 04900 (U) Christopher Wren Inc			1,388.43
5831	29 23 28 4075 05400 (U) Riley Maureen S & Welch James Douglas			2,234.85
5832	29 23 28 4075 05430 (U) Mazza Joseph D &			
5968	03 24 28 7841 00200 (U) Aurell Stanley O & Aurell Margery J		HX	2,913.28
5969	03 24 28 7841 00330 (U) Dupuis Gilles P & Dupuis Michele L			3,775.76
5970	03 24 28 7841 00390 (U) Kim David		HX	5,865.09
5971	03 24 28 7841 00500 (U) Reyes Jon & Reyes Shirley		HX	5,445.43
5972	03 24 28 7841 00550 (U) Antonov Stoimen & Antonov Anna		HX	3,303.53
5973	04 24 28 0000 00010 (U) Viola Frank S Jr & Viola Kathy M		HX	70,961.87
5974	04 24 28 0000 00039 (U) Mercado Perez Miguel A & Santiago Bonet Damaris G			12,856.67
5975	04 24 28 0000 00050 (U) Kasu Abdul Ghani & Kasu Sayeeda		HX	9,749.31
5976	04 24 28 0000 00107 (U) Haddad Iaal & Haddad Mylene			14,501.14
Lake Nona Ph 1 A Parcel 6				
17869	07 24 31 4749 00060 (A) Burton Michael & Burton Lorna			36,260.27
17870	07 24 31 4749 00090 (A) Smee Roger G			12,066.97
17871	07 24 31 4749 00110 (A) Oliver Vernon J & Neaves Mary Jane.			14,374.01
Lake Nona Ph 1 A Parcel 7				
17872	07 24 31 4750 00150 (A) Wilkins J Dominique & Wilkins Nicole R			4,167.79
17873	07 24 31 4750 00160 (A) Wilkins J Dominique & Wilkins Nicole R			4,154.87
17874	07 24 31 4750 00310 (A) Pierce Russell & Pierce Alison			5,487.10
Live Oak Ests Ph 2				
17875	14 24 31 5109 00020 (U) Gresham Lawrence & Gresham Carolyn &		HX	3,769.51

misunderstand, the bank remains liable for the property taxes, it just delays paying them until it can find a buyer for the property.

At one sale a few years ago, I saw four houses from my own neighborhood listed in the tax lien list. Figure 2.10 will give you some idea

FIGURE 2.7 *Sports Star Property Liens (Continued)*

17859	07 24 31 4710 00100	(A)	Isayama Chiyoko	6,813.62
Lake Nona Ph 1 A Parcel 9			
17860	07 24 31 4711 00150	(A)	Shoffer Lawrence J & Shoffer Kathleen B	29,213.78
17861	07 24 31 4711 00380	(A)	Faldo Nicholas A C/O Chris Hubman	5,130.20
17862	07 24 31 4711 00390	(A)	Faldo Nicholas A C/O Chris Hubman	5,130.20
Lake Nona Ph 1 A Parcel 4 Rep			
17863	07 24 31 4713 00050	(A)	De Voogel Douglas P & De Voogel Lisa Marie	29,969.96
17864	07 24 31 4713 00100	(A)	Fryer John A E & Fryer June	16,203.78

Isleworth

5509	16 23 28 3899 00790	(U)	Bre Capital Group Inc	9,535.20
5510	16 23 28 3899 01030	(U)	Carter Butch	20,537.97
5511	16 23 28 3899 01150	(U)	Gonzalez Juan	HX 22,874.26
5512	16 23 28 3899 01480	(U)	Omicrom Investments Ltd	60,437.55
5513	16 23 28 3899 01500	(U)	Kay Christopher K & Kay Kristine K	HX 18,100.92
5514	16 23 28 3899 01730	(U)	Scott Dennis E	27,620.23
5515	16 23 28 3899 01770	(U)	Harding Victor H & Harding Deborah Lynn	HX 23,825.96
5516	16 23 28 3899 02980	(U)	Tominaga Yasuhiko & Tominaga Yoko	HX 14,172.63
5517	16 23 28 3899 03030	(U)	Levin Jackie Renault House	15 774 52

5815	29 23 28 4074 01680	(U)	Hanning Franz S & Hanning Kelly M	25,708.19
5816	29 23 28 4074 01690	(U)	Blake Jeffrey C & Blake Lewanna	12,709.24
5817	29 23 28 4074 01800	(U)	Varroux Alan R & Varroux Lorraine P	12,867.22
5818	29 23 28 4074 01890	(U)	Hamilton Thomas E & Hamilton Jackie C	HX 6,881.14
5819	29 23 28 4074 01960	(U)	Griffey George K &	

of how nice these properties are. I was shocked. This is a small, gated community with only 16 homes. Most of the properties are now valued at $750,000 to over a million dollars. Twenty-five percent of my

FIGURE 2.7 *Sports Star Property Liens (Continued)*

ERNESTO GONZALEZ &W ELIA M
$7916.29
11643 02 32270100140
ANNA KOURNIKOVA & $106178.89
11644 02 32270100280
GARY VIOLET &W VIOLA $21994.94
11645 02 32270100290

HERBERT D MENDEL TR
11693 02 32
CHARLES E SOFGE
11694 02 32
RAFAEL A GIL
11695 02 32
DOLPHIN ENTERPRISES II I

EDGAR HOFFMAN CLAVIER $11228.15
11704 02 32320060370
THE ROYAL BAY GROUP LLC$18998.09
11705 02 32320060570
STEFANIE GRAF $17090.63
11706 02 32320060600
PEDRO O RODRIGUEZ &W ANA V
$79250.55
11707 02 32320060850
ROYAL BAY ESTATES AT SOUTH

JOSE & ROBERTO SANTANA $2220.8
11754 02 3233037040
JUAN MIGUEL REVELLO $824.8
11755 02 3233037048
ALBERTO E VILLEGAS &W OLGA C
$2271.7
11756 02 3233038008
JACK ALEXANDER HARTLEY $3299.5
11757 02 3233038009
DENISE RICHARD &W SUSAN $3137.3

neighborhood had tax liens on them! As you can see, I lived in a bad neighborhood!

Can't these people pay their property taxes? I suppose they can. I can only tell you why I think these four properties had

FIGURE 2.8 *Celebrity Property Liens*

5100	34 22 28 0117 00050 (U)	Anderson William L &		
		Anderson Debra L	HX	3,489.
5101	34 22 28 0117 00330 (U)	Buchta Larry J &		
		Buchta Dorothy J	HX	2,559.8
5102	34 22 28 0117 00690 (U)	Peake Donna		3,237.5
5103	34 22 28 0117 05000 (U)	Almond Tree Estates Inc		
		C/O Angelia Gordon Property Mngt Inc		139.7
Hamptons				
5104	34 22 28 3313 00280 (U)	Murcia Blanca L	HX	2,903.4
5105	34 22 28 3313 00290 (U)	Snipes Marion J & Snipes Wesley		4,943.0

14016	05 22 30 6654 04407 (B)	W P Park West Llc	754.05
Sylvan Park			
14017	05 22 30 8502 0121 (B)	Carrot Top Inc	4,683.65
Sylvan Park Rep			
14018	05 22 30 8503 00100 (B)	Gray Michael L & Gray Wendy P	4,434.99
Sylvan Hgts			
14019	05 22 30 8504 02072 (B)	Sims Leger Lien Hoa	2,470.51
14020	05 22 30 8504 04031 (B)	Salvation Army	476.93
14021	05 22 30 8504 04040 (B)	Taylor Scott M	2,296.62
14022	05 22 30 8504 04070 (B)	Razzani Russell A	HX 1,721.96

delinquent taxes on them. Two houses were in foreclosure (same owner), one involved a divorce, and one had an out-of-the-country owner. There are always a multitude of reasons why property taxes are not timely paid.

In Figure 2.11, you'll see various commercial properties on which I've bought liens.

FIGURE 2.9 *Julius Erving's Condos*

So let me now ask you, Do you think these liens occur only on "crack" houses?

LARRY'S REMINDERS

- All properties (other than Indian reservations) incur property taxes. These taxes pay for local police and fire service, schools, libraries, roads, and salaries of local officials.
- Tax liens can be found on all kinds of properties—vacant lots, small houses, luxury homes, condos, commercial properties, shopping centers, and industrial properties. At any given sale, you may find liens on well-known companies, athletes, and even other government agencies.
- Lien amounts range from $100 to over $1 million.

FIGURE 2.10 *Four Examples of Residential Tax Lien Properties*

FIGURE 2.11 *Commercial Properties with Tax Liens*

3

10 PERCENT TO 300 PERCENT RETURNS—AND THIS IS SAFE?

"I think stocks will be a great way to make 6 or 7 percent a year for the next 10 or 15 years. But anyone who expects 15 percent a year is living in a dream world."
WARREN BUFFETT

From 1926 to 2000, the stock market averaged 11 percent growth annually (*First Union Perspective*, May 2001). However, as First Union (now Wachovia) points out, the market did not main tain that growth on a steady and consistent basis. Says First Union: "In some years, the market will gain more or less than the average, and in some years it will post losses."

Indeed, years 2000–2002 were horrible years for stock market investors. In fact, according to *USA Today* (March 2-4, 2001), in 2000 the Nasdaq stock index dropped 39.3 percent. If you had invested your money on Nasdaq stocks, on average, you would have *lost* 39 percent of your money! Even the "rock solid" S&P 500 lost 10 percent! As such, an individual investing in the market at the beginning of year 2000 would likely need several years to recoup his or her principal! Perhaps even more startling was the revelation on April 29, 2001, of billionaire Warren Buffett, easily the most-respected name on Wall Street. In front of 17,000 listeners, Buffett stated: "I think stocks will be a great way to make 6 or 7 percent a year for the next 10 or 15 years. But anyone who expects

15 percent a year is living in a dream world" (*Chicago Tribune,* April 30, 2001).

Buffett's prognostication turned out to be optimistic, at least for 2001 and 2002. While 2003 and 2004 showed that the market had rebounded, the damage to portfolios and retirement accounts from the 2000 to 2002 years was overwhelming. *USA Today* revealed that the S&P 500 lost another 13 percent in 2001 and 23.4 percent in 2002, while the Nasdaq lost another 21.1 percent in 2001 and 31.5 percent in 2002 (January 2, 2003). Rock-solid companies like Coca-Cola and General Electric lost half of their value. Fortunes were lost and were not coming back any time soon. In fact, an article by *Business Week* on March 14, 2003, indicated that many investors in blue chip stocks who came into the market near its peak in 1999 might not recoup their principal for decades. Take a look at these respected companies and how long it may take an investor simply to regain his or her principal, assuming a 7 percent annual growth rate:

	Years to Recover
Microsoft	15
Intel	23
Amazon.com	23
AOL Time Warner	27
Yahoo	38
Sun Microsystems	45
Lucent Technologies	55

While the stock market recovered and posted decent returns from 2003 through 2005, many stocks only recovered to their 1999 highs. The market was good in 2006, but 2007 has been quite volatile. Having been bludgeoned in the stock market, many investors are looking for a safe haven where they can park their money. Unfortunately, the typical choice for most Americans looking for a safe, short-term investment is to purchase a certificate of deposit.

At the time of this writing, however, CDs are paying about 5 percent, depending on the maturity. Bonds and gold investments have been two other choices for safe-haven investing, but even these investments carry inherent risk. (See "Investors Finding Fewer Safe Havens," *USA Today,* March 5, 2003, and "Bonds: The Risks of Rising Rates," *Business Week,* April 21, 2003.)

Where do investors turn when looking for a decent yield and a fair amount of safety? Is it possible to achieve a safe, steady, and reliable 8 to 15 percent, or even more? Indeed it is! As indicated in Chapter 1, tax lien certificates provide these types of reliable returns with the following safety benefits:

- They are administered by the government.
- They are secured by real estate.
- They are enforced by state law.
- Their rates are fixed.

Consider the chart in Figure 3.1. Notice the possible returns according to state jurisdiction. Keep in mind that these are only the better lien and hybrid states listed. See Part 3 for a complete list of states. In addition, keep in mind that many of the states listed are "bid down the interest" jurisdictions, which means that the bidding starts at a statutory maximum rate but may be bid down to as little as $\frac{1}{4}$ percent.

Let's start with the downside. In "bid down the interest" states like Florida, Illinois, and the District of Columbia, the statutory rate may be 18 percent, but that is only where the bidding begins. Most liens on good properties will be bid well below that now, since other investments are offering less than 5 percent. In most "bid down" jurisdictions, the rate is commonly bid down to 6 to 9 percent. In Florida, the rate will be bid down considerably lower. Since rates on "safe" investments like certificates of deposit are so low, institutional bidders have been bidding most good Florida properties down to $\frac{1}{4}$ percent. For the novice investor this action doesn't make any sense. Why would these institutional bidders

FIGURE 3.1 *Possible Returns on Tax Liens*

State	Statutory Rate	Maximum Return[1]
1. Texas[2]	25%	300%
2. Georgia	20	240
3. Illinois	18	216
4. Delaware[3]	15	180
5. Rhode Island	16	120
6. Indiana[4]	15	120
7. New Jersey[5]	19	90
8. Louisiana	13.7	72
9. Florida[6]	18	60
10. Wyoming	15.75	51
11. Montana	12	34
12. Iowa	24	24
13. Maryland[7]	12–20	20
14. Connecticut	18	18
15. Mississippi	18	18
16. New Hampshire	18	18
17. Ohio	18	18
18. District of Columbia[8]	18	18

[1]The maximum rate of return is determined by a redemption date of one month after the sale, where penalty states are concerned. If redemption occurs faster than one month, those states would show an even higher rate of return.

[2]Texas has a 25 percent penalty and six-month redemption period for nonhomestead, nonagricultural property (shown). For homestead or agricultural properties, the redemption period is two years and the penalty is 25 percent for year one and 50 percent for year two.

[3]Varies by county.

[4]Indiana is a premium bidding state that applies a penalty return. However, on any overbid (i.e., premium over the lien amount), the investor will receive only 10 percent simple interest (with the penalty applied to the lien amount).

[5]New Jersey is a "bid down the interest" state, starting at 18 percent. However, it also adds a penalty based on the size of the lien. Liens under $4,999 have an additional 2 percent penalty, liens from $5,000 to $9,999 have an additional 4 percent penalty, and liens of $10,000 and over have an additional 6 percent penalty. Both figures assume you got the lien under $5,000 and a redemption of two years. The maximum was based on a lien over $10,000 and redemption after one month.

[6]Florida is a "bid down the interest" state, starting at 18 percent. In addition, Florida has a minimum 5 percent penalty (thus, a lien paying off after one month receives a 60 percent rate of return).

[7]Varies by county. Several counties have a rate of 20 percent.

[8]The District of Columbia uses premium bidding (and the investor gets no interest on the premium). When this occurs, the rate of return is reduced.

accept a rate so low? The answer lies in the difference between an interest rate and a yield, or rate of return.

Let's say, for example, that I buy a lien in Florida at a rate of ¼ percent. My *yield,* or rate of return, is likely to be around 8 to 10 percent. This is the part that the novice investor misses altogether. Florida has a minimum penalty of 5 percent. As such, even if I bid 1 percent, the minimum penalty to the owner is 5 percent. If the owner pays the lien off one year later, do I get 1 percent or 5 percent? I would receive 5 percent, since that is the minimum.

Can you see that the state inserted this penalty as a safety net for investors? This penalty makes it worthwhile for the investor and also ensures that the county will sell all of its liens. Now let's continue the math. If the investor paid off the lien in one month, what is my rate of return? Since I'll get a 5 percent penalty in one month, that's a 60 percent rate of return ($5 \times 12 = 60$). And if the owner paid off in two months, that's a 30 percent return.

Now let's assume the investor bought 100 liens at a sale. Recall that Florida's redemption period is two years. As such, the investor bidding very low has a risk that some liens will pay off late in the redemption period. For example, if a lien paid off in the 24th month, the minimum 5 percent penalty would only give the investor a return of 2½ percent per year. However, institutional bidders realize that liens will redeem all throughout the redemption period. Some will redeem after 1 month, 2 months, 10 months, 15 months, and so on. Out of 100 liens, you can be assured that liens will redeem every month or so over the two-year period. In addition, many liens on very nice properties tend to redeem faster. As such, the investor will get returns of 60 percent on some liens, 30 percent on some liens, 20 percent on some liens, and, yes, 5 or 2½ percent on other liens.

Here's the second point about those institutional bidders going down to ¼ percent. For those liens that do not redeem, the investor will file for a tax deed (more on that in Chapter 6). In doing so, the investor must buy out the other lien holder (recall a two-year redemption period) at the rate that investor bid and pay the county a processing fee. The county will now take both certificates (his and the other lien holder's) and give the investor a new certificate, at a new interest rate of 18 percent. This aggregate lien will accrue at 18 percent until the tax deed sale, some four to six months away. If you account for some liens paying off quickly and others going to tax deed sale, you will now see why these bidders go down to ¼ percent at the sale. On average, their yield is in the range of 8 to 10 percent. In today's market, to get that yield safely is very attractive.

The good news, of course, is that in every case the investor is choosing the return that is acceptable. If the bidding goes down below the investor's acceptable rate, he or she simply drops out of the bidding and waits on the next lien. In Chapter 5, I'll discuss the different types of bidding systems and how always to get the best rates.

Now for the better news. First, some lien states have a flat rate. For example, Iowa pays a flat 2 percent per month. On an annualized basis, that's a fixed 24 percent per year! Any complaints? Maryland counties have flat rates that range from 12 to 20 percent. The best states, Texas and Georgia, however, are hybrid states and do not have interest rates but penalties. For example, in Texas the penalty is 25 percent and in Georgia, 20 percent. But that rate is neither an interest rate nor a yield, since the penalty is the same regardless of when it is paid. Suppose, for example, that I promise you a 25 percent per annum interest rate on a loan of $10,000. At the end of 12 months, I would owe you $2,500 interest plus the principal, right? At the end of six months, it would be $1,250. At the end of one month, $208.33.

Now let's switch to a 25 percent *penalty*. At the end of one year I owe you $2,500, just like the interest rate. But at the end of six months I still owe you $2,500. And at the end of one month I still owe you $2,500. What is your rate of return, or *yield*, if I pay you the $2,500 in just six months? Fifty percent. What is your yield if I pay you in just one month? *Three hundred* percent!

Now let's apply what we've learned about yields to Texas. If you invest in a Texas deed (recall that it is a hybrid state), the redemption period is either six months for nonhomestead, nonagricultural properties, or two years for a homestead or agricultural property. If the former, that means you have a 25 percent penalty with a six-month redemption period. If the owner redeems at the end of the six-month period, what is your rate of return? Fifty percent! What if the owner redeems after two months? One hundred fifty percent! One month? Three hundred percent!

Now I know what you are thinking: *Yes, that's great, but I still have to reinvest my money again.* Yes, you have to reinvest, but you have made a phenomenal yield, safely, and you can reinvest that money again in more deeds or in some other investment. If you just put the money under your bed, you'd still have a 25 percent yield for the year. My guess is that you wouldn't put the money under your bed but would reinvest it in another deed, lien, or other investment as soon as you received the cash. The good news for Texas is that deed sales occur monthly.

From the tax lien/deed investor's standpoint, penalties offer substantial benefits. In addition to hybrid states, some lien states also add penalties to their interest rates. For example, New Jersey is a "bid down the interest" state, starting at 18 percent. However, the state also adds a 2 to 4 percent penalty, depending on the size of the lien. In Part 3, I'll break down how each state works so you can see the impact of the interest, penalty, and redemption period rules.

I was speaking at a seminar some time ago and someone asked me afterward, "What is the best rate of return you have received on a lien?" I smiled. They guessed, "One hundred percent?" I smiled again. "Two hundred percent?" "Higher," I said. "Five hundred percent?" I smiled and again said, "Higher." "What," they said, "that's impossible."

While this return and scenario is not too common, it does occur. I'll give you the story and you figure out my rate of return. While Florida offers an interest rate (rather than a penalty), recall the minimum 5 percent return. That is, regardless of the interest rate at which you bought the lien, the state will make sure that the minimum you receive is 5 percent. I gave a brief rationale earlier why the state does this, but let's apply it.

Let's assume you bought a lien at 12 percent interest. Not a bad rate of return. But what if the owner redeems and pays it off after one month. What is the amount of interest you receive? Only 1 percent, right? If you bought a $2,000 lien, that's only $20 and is not really worth your while. So the legislature made it a little more palatable by requiring a minimum 5 percent penalty. On this lien, that is only $100, but it helps.

Now let's apply the Florida rule to the following scenario. At the annual sale in Orange County, Florida, the county requires a $1,000 deposit to bid and invoices the investor for amounts due beyond that after the sale (or sends a refund of the balance due if the investor buys less than $1,000 in liens). In Orlando, the tax lien auction is held near the end of May (typically May 24–28). Since I typically buy more than $1,000 in liens, the Tax Collector invoices me for the balance due about two weeks later. One particular year, the deadline for payment was June 12, as I recall. When I went in to the Tax Collector's office to pay the invoice, I noticed that I had a check in the packet the office assistant gave to me. Seeing the check, I said, "What's this?" "Oh, one of your liens redeemed," she said. It was a check for one of the liens I had purchased; the owner had redeemed and paid off the lien with the 5 percent penalty.

Let's do the math. If I received the 5 percent penalty one month after buying a lien, what would be my yield? Sixty percent (5 ×12 = 60). Recall, however, that this check came in, with my 5 percent penalty, *before* I had actually paid for the lien! So what is my rate of return? Sixty percent? Higher. One hundred percent? Higher. Five hundred percent? Higher. Since I had not actually purchased the lien before I was paid a return, my rate of return would be *infinite*!

I'm often asked, "What's the best state to invest in?" That's like asking where you can find the best pizza. Ask someone from Chicago and someone from New York, and you'll likely get different answers. Once you've got the right city, then you have to choose the best restaurant. This investment scenario is much the same. What's the best state? That depends on your answers to these questions:

- Do you want to invest in liens or deeds?
- If you want to invest in liens, are you willing to invest in hybrid states?
- Where do you reside?
- Are you willing to travel to another state to invest? (While a few states now allow online bidding, I caution you against doing so in an area with which you are unfamiliar.)
- How much do you have to spend?
- Are you willing to do research?
- If you travel to another state, do you realize that you must deduct your expenses from your yield unless you are going there anyway?

I also usually tell people that they can invest based on one of these five options:

1. Invest in your local jurisdiction because it is close and easy.
2. Invest in the jurisdiction that pays the best rates.
3. Invest in the jurisdiction where your relatives live (i.e., you go there anyway).
4. Invest in the jurisdiction where you like to vacation.
5. Invest in the jurisdiction where you can own the property for the best price (i.e., deed sale).

Now let's look at possible answers to these questions. Suppose you tell me that you just want something simple and the best rate of return. I'll tell you to invest in Iowa, since it pays 2 percent per month. But if you live in Florida or California, there will be a plane fare, hotel, and rental car to deduct from your yield. If you live in California and don't have relatives in Iowa, I'll tell you to go to Phoenix and invest in an Arizona lien (16 percent, but a bid down jurisdiction). If you tell me you just want the best return and are willing to do some research, I'll tell you to go to Texas. If you tell me you want to acquire properties for as little as possible, I'll tell you to invest in Kansas or buy liens on properties whose redemption periods have already expired (more on that in Chapter 10).

Keep in mind also that one county may be substantially better (based on crowds or local rules) than the county next door, even though they are in the same state. You also may want to consider investing in jurisdictions that have online sales (but do this in areas that you know well). There are so many variables to consider, the right investment jurisdiction will vary for each investor. My suggestion is to answer the questions above and look at the details of each state in Part 3.

LARRY'S REMINDERS

- Tax lien investing offers safe and reliable returns of 8 to 15 percent, and, in some jurisdictions, much more.
- Tax lien investing offers the following safety benefits:
  —They are administered by the government.
  —They are secured by real estate.
  —They are enforced by state law.
  —Their rates are fixed.
- Understand the difference between an interest rate (per annum) and a yield, which is your actual rate of return for any given period.
- Jurisdictions that have penalties will significantly increase your yield.
- There is no "best" state. Each state has pros and cons for investors, and each investor has specific needs, wants, and goals. Review the list of states in Part 3 to determine which is best for you.

4

THE AUCTION
Rules, Dates, and Fees

Most lien states will have an annual auction, while deed and hybrid deed states typically have their sales more often. For example, California has biannual sales. Georgia and Texas, both hybrid states, conduct their sales on a monthly basis. Larger counties in Pennsylvania typically hold their deed sales *weekly*!

Keep in mind that a lien state also may have deed sales. For example, Florida, a lien state, also conducts deed sales, since a lien not redeemed requires the lien holder to have the property sold at a deed sale to pay off the lien. In smaller Florida counties, these deed sales will occur quarterly or bimonthly, while larger counties will have monthly deed sales. Orange County, Florida, typically will have two sales per month but may have as many as four sales in a month! The rules and regulations for these auctions vary by state and also by county. You will need to contact the specific county to review its rules.

The remaining information in this section will largely apply to lien jurisdictions. For more information on deed auctions, see Chapters 8 to 13.

FEES

Few counties charge a fee for the right to bid at their auctions, although some of the larger counties do so. For example, Woodbury County, Iowa (second largest in the state), charged a $75 fee the last time I was there, while Polk County (Des Moines), Iowa (largest in the state), charged a $100 fee. All of the other Iowa counties that I've been to, however, do not charge a fee. Florida counties do not charge a fee, but many require a $1,000 deposit before bidding. The District of Columbia requires a deposit of 20 percent of what you expect to buy at the auction. Indianapolis, Indiana, charges no fee and requires no deposit. Deed auctions typically do not require fees or deposits, although larger counties may require a minimum deposit. Los Angeles County, California, for example, requires a deposit of $1,000 before you are allowed to bid at the annual auction. If a county requires a deposit and you spend less than that amount, the county will mail you a check for the difference.

I know what a few of you may be thinking at this point: *To have better odds of getting a lot of good liens, can I have more than one bidder card at the auction?* Indeed, you may have more than one card. However, most counties will limit you in several ways. First, you must pay your fee or deposit per bidder card. Second, each bidder card must be represented by a different Social Security number or tax identification number (i.e., a corporate or retirement account purchase). Third, many counties will give you only one bidder card per person in the auction. For example, say you have one bidder card representing you personally (with your Social Security number on the W-9) and another card representing your corporation (with its tax identification number on the W-9). Many counties will let you take only one card in at a time. If you bring a friend to hold one card, that solves the problem. Otherwise, when you have finished buying for one card, you must return that card to the county and then go back into the auction room with the second card. This is really not a problem, and I've done it many times; however, you need to know this rule before you try to walk in with two cards at one time. If the county is conducting its sale online, you still need to register for each bidder number with a tax identification or Social Security number.

AUCTION DATES

A disadvantage of lien states, however, is that the auction only comes once a year. For example, you may decide to invest in Iowa liens because of the outstanding rate of 2 percent per month. However, the auctions are all held in June. So what do you do when some of your liens redeem and you want to keep them earning interest? Ideally, you immediately invest in another lien in another state. Since lien sales are held virtually every month of the year, you can keep reinvesting. The problem, of course, is that you don't want to travel to each jurisdiction every time you want to buy another lien. While a few counties have adopted online bidding, most counties still require a warm body in the auction room.

A second potential disadvantage to live auction lien investing is that some counties may be holding their auctions on exactly the same date, and you cannot be in two places at one time, unless you send a friend or family member to one auction and you attend the other. (Note that this isn't a problem if the county allows online bidding, as you put in your bid ahead of time.) As such, you may be able to visit only one county auction for that month or year. For example, all of the Iowa counties pay the 2 percent per month, but the lien auctions all start on the same day! When I bought liens in Iowa, I reviewed lien lists and spoke to the County Treasurers in Shelby, Monoma, Harrison, and Woodbury counties. I was able to attend, however, only auctions at Shelby, Woodbury, and Polk counties. In case you are wondering how I managed to get in three counties, here was my schedule:

Monday morning—Attend Shelby County sale (smallest county).

Monday afternoon—Drive to and attend Woodbury County sale.

Tuesday morning—Drive to Des Moines (Polk County).

Tuesday afternoon—Attend Polk County sale.

Since smaller counties like Shelby, Monoma, and Harrison would be finished in two hours or less, I had to choose one to attend first. I knew that Woodbury County was large enough to have its sale continue well into the afternoon, so I attended that sale second. Since the Polk County sale would continue to a second or third day, I attended that sale third. There is somewhat of a strategy here, because smaller counties have fewer bidders but also fewer liens. By my estimates, Shelby County had only 20 bidders but only about 75 liens available; Woodbury had about 100 bidders and about 1,500 liens available; and Des Moines had 300 to 400 bidders with several thousand liens available.

Florida auctions take place in late May and early June. The larger counties will hold an auction for one to three weeks, while the smaller counties will hold the auction in two to four days. Since there are 67 counties in Florida, an investor can literally jump around the state to invest more money. In reality, however, only the institutional bidders that have millions and millions to invest do this. Most individual investors will run out of money to spend at one county. The good news for those who don't like to travel is that most of the large Florida counties have changed their auctions to online only.

ONLINE INVESTING

When I wrote the first edition of this book in 2004, online bidding was a novel concept. One city in California (Bakersfield, Kern County) was doing it, and the larger cities in Florida were going to try it. I predicted then that more counties would be using that method to sell liens in the future. It only made sense. In my county, the tax assessor's office had to rent a huge auditorium for a week, have a half-dozen county employees at the sale, and employ "spotters" for a week. The auditorium alone would cost tens of thousands of dollars. If all bidding was conducted online, however, the county wouldn't pay a penny to rent space (although they would incur some software programming costs).

Today, every major city in Florida sells liens through online bidding. However, this sale method has not become a national trend. Outside of Florida, only a few counties are using it (see List of States). I'm actually happy about that because, as I mentioned earlier, you can't use any "tricks of the trade" if the bidding is online. Since online bidding has existed for several years now, I don't expect many more counties will switch to it if they haven't already. For the small investor and those who want higher yields, that's good news.

From the investor's standpoint, there are pros and cons to having an online sale. The benefit is for people who want to invest in another region of the state or country. Instead of actually going there, now they can buy liens over the Internet during the sale week. Someone with a lot of money can be buying liens in several counties simultaneously. The downside is that small, local buyers will likely have additional competition. Second, since bids are placed ahead of time, you really don't have a chance to watch the "feel" of how the bidding is going.

I first bought liens online in 2004 at the auction for Orange County, Florida (Orlando). The system Orlando uses is the same as in other major Florida cities. Here's how it works in Florida.

The county directs you to register for the sale at a specific Web site. You then mail the county a check for $1,000 per bidder number. All liens are listed on the site with lien amount and parcel identification number (allowing you to cross-reference to the appraiser's office). Once registered, you type in a bid percentage next to the lien you desire. See Figure 4.1. When the auction starts, the computer system awards the lien to the bidder with the lowest percentage (bid down system). If two bidders have the same percentage, the computer picks are at random.

FIGURE 4.1 *Orange County Online Auction*

Honorable Earl K. Wood

BidOrangeCounty.com

TAX CERTIFICATE AUCTION WEB SITE

Summary	Search	Reports	Budgets	Bid	Results	Upload/Download	My Ac

You Are: Larry Loftis   Bidder ID: BUYR-LE (# 305)   Last Update: 5:02:43 p

Refresh

Total Security Deposits	Maximum Allowable Budget	Actual Budget Variance (Over/Under Allowable)
$1,000.00	$10,000.00	$0.00

Make Payment

Save Budgets   **Total Budget:** $10,000.00
Budget Used: $0.00
Budget Remaining: $10,000.00

Batch #	Adv #'s	Award Time	Total Submitted Bids	Batch Budgets
1	1 - 1000	May 19, 2004 9:00 am EDT	$ —	$
2	1001 - 2000	May 19, 2004 10:00 am EDT	$ —	$
3	2001 - 3000	May 19, 2004 11:00 am EDT	$ —	$
4	3001 - 4000	May 19, 2004 12:00 pm EDT	$ —	$
5	4001 - 5000	May 19, 2004 1:00 pm EDT	$ —	$
6	5001 - 6000	May 19, 2004 2:00 pm EDT	$ —	$
7	6001 - 7000	May 19, 2004 3:00 pm EDT	$ —	$
8	7001 - 8000	May 19, 2004 4:00 pm EDT	$ —	$
9	8001 - 9000	May 20, 2004 9:00 am EDT	$ —	$
10	9001 - 10000	May 20, 2004 10:00 am EDT	$ —	$
11	10001 - 11000	May 20, 2004 11:00 am EDT	$ —	$
12	11001 - 12000	May 20, 2004 12:00 pm EDT	$ —	$
13	12001 - 13000	May 20, 2004 1:00 pm EDT	$ —	$
14	13001 - 14000	May 20, 2004 2:00 pm EDT	$ —	$
15	14001 - 15000	May 20, 2004 3:00 pm EDT	$ —	$
16	15001 - 16000	May 20, 2004 4:00 pm EDT	$ —	$
17	16001 - 17000	May 21, 2004 9:00 am EDT	$ —	$
18	17001 - 18000	May 21, 2004 10:00 am EDT	$ —	$
19	18001 - 19000	May 21, 2004 11:00 am EDT	$ —	$
20	19001 - 20000	May 21, 2004 12:00 pm EDT	$ —	$
21	20001 - 20231	May 21, 2004 1:00 pm EDT	$ —	$
Save Budgets		Totals:	$ —	$ —

The online system actually has one surprising benefit. Let's say you bid $\frac{1}{4}$ percent and the next lowest bid was $8\frac{1}{4}$ percent. Because you would only go to 8 percent at a live auction, the computer system awards you the lien at 8 percent. However, because most liens on good properties in my county are now bid at $\frac{1}{4}$ percent by the institutional bidders (see Chapter 3 for why), some bidders (e.g., Wachovia, Atlantic Bank) may have over a dozen bids at $\frac{1}{4}$ percent. As such, if you have two bids at $\frac{1}{4}$ and the next lowest bid is 8 percent, the computer only sees two bidders at $\frac{1}{4}$ and will give you that item at $\frac{1}{4}$ rather than $7\frac{3}{4}$ (it has happened to me!).

Online auctions are here to stay, at least for the counties now using this method (see List of States to see which state and counties are now using online bidding). For the investor, online auctions have advantages and disadvantages. For county administrators and tax collectors, however, online auctions have virtually no downside.

A STRATEGY FOR THE BIGGER PLAYERS

Want more liens? Recall that the county is going to give one bidder card per Social Security number or tax identification number. If your county is using a "random selection" or "rotational" bidding process (see Chapter 5), the more cards you have in the auction (or online), the better chances you will have to purchase excellent liens. I typically will use one card for my personal investments and another card for my corporate purchases. With this strategy, I have better odds of getting more liens. Some investors use multiple corporations and/or children's and spouse's Social Security numbers to acquire multiple bidder numbers.

At the Shelby County, Iowa, sale I attended a few years ago, for example, there were 22 bidder cards issued. However, one individual had some 8 numbers (held by family members). He had the opportunity to buy over one-third of the liens offered! At the Woodbury sale, one individual had 20 numbers (held by individuals who were hired for one day to do so). Once these bidders acquired liens for their "boss" (likely using their own Social Security numbers), they would typically assign them to their boss (most counties charge $2 to $10 to do so).

You may want to consider using two cards (assuming it's not an online auction), even in "bid down" jurisdictions. Here's why. At live auctions, many counties get behind on their timetable and have to "catch up." The county tax collector or treasurer has rented a commercial facility to conduct the auction for, say, one week. The county official knows that to finish on time he or she must complete one fifth of the liens for sale each day. In many cases, if the county gets behind, the county official conducting the sale will begin to start "picking" numbers quickly (or limit bidding to just a few seconds) in order to move through liens and catch up. When this happens, it means the county has just unofficially moved from a "bid down" system to a "random selection" system! Thus, the more cards you have in the room, the better your chances.

REGISTRATION

All counties require registration prior to your investing at a lien auction. The reason for this is because the county will be reporting the interest you receive to the Internal Revenue Service. Typically, this registration just means filling out a W-9 form for each Social Security or tax identification number and a bidder registration form (see Figure 4.2). Because most auctions commence in the morning, you should register at least one day in advance. Keep in mind that some counties may require you to register well in advance of the auction. At the Los Angeles deed auction, for example, the county requires registration a week before the auction. You'll need to speak with the county in advance to review its registration policy. In most lien jurisdictions, the county will allow you to register at the sale itself (unless it's an online auction, of course) during any auction day.

FIGURE 4.2 *Taxpayer Identification Form W-9*

Form W-9
(Rev. January 2003)
Department of the Treasury
Internal Revenue Service

Request for Taxpayer Identification Number and Certification

Give form to the requester. Do not send to the IRS.

See Specific Instructions on page 2.
Print or type

Name

Business name, if different from above

Check appropriate box: ☐ Individual/Sole proprietor ☐ Corporation ☐ Partnership ☐ Other ▶ .... ☐ Exempt from backup withholding

Address (number, street, and apt. or suite no.)

Requester's name and address (optional)

City, state, and ZIP code

List account number(s) here (optional)

Part I **Taxpayer Identification Number (TIN)**

Enter your TIN in the appropriate box. For individuals, this is your social security number (SSN). **However, for a resident alien, sole proprietor, or disregarded entity, see the Part I instructions on page 3.** For other entities, it is your employer identification number (EIN). If you do not have a number, see **How to get a TIN** on page 3.

Note: *If the account is in more than one name, see the chart on page 4 for guidelines on whose number to enter.*

Social security number

or

Employer identification number

Part II **Certification**

Under penalties of perjury, I certify that:

1. The number shown on this form is my correct taxpayer identification number (or I am waiting for a number to be issued to me), **and**

2. I am not subject to backup withholding because: **(a)** I am exempt from backup withholding, or **(b)** I have not been notified by the Internal Revenue Service (IRS) that I am subject to backup withholding as a result of a failure to report all interest or dividends, or **(c)** the IRS has notified me that I am no longer subject to backup withholding, **and**

3. I am a U.S. person (including a U.S. resident alien).

Certification instructions. You must cross out item **2** above if you have been notified by the IRS that you are currently subject to backup withholding because you have failed to report all interest and dividends on your tax return. For real estate transactions, item **2** does not apply. For mortgage interest paid, acquisition or abandonment of secured property, cancellation of debt, contributions to an individual retirement arrangement (IRA), and generally, payments other than interest and dividends, you are not required to sign the Certification, but you must provide your correct TIN. (See the instructions on page 4.)

Sign Here

Signature of U.S. person ▶

Date ▶

Purpose of Form

A person who is required to file an information return with the IRS, must obtain your correct taxpayer identification number (TIN) to report, for example, income paid to you, real estate transactions, mortgage interest you paid, acquisition or abandonment of secured property, cancellation of debt, or contributions you made to an IRA.

U.S. person. Use Form W-9 only if you are a U.S. person (including a resident alien), to provide your correct TIN to the person requesting it (the requester) and, when applicable, to:

1. Certify that the TIN you are giving is correct (or you are waiting for a number to be issued),

2. Certify that you are not subject to backup withholding, or

3. Claim exemption from backup withholding if you are a U.S. exempt payee.

Note: *If a requester gives you a form other than Form W-9 to request your TIN, you must use the requester's form if it is substantially similar to this Form W-9.*

Foreign person. If you are a foreign person, use the appropriate Form W-8 (see **Pub. 515,** Withholding of Tax on Nonresident Aliens and Foreign Entities).

Nonresident alien who becomes a resident alien. Generally, only a nonresident alien individual may use the terms of a tax treaty to reduce or eliminate U.S. tax on certain types of income. However, most tax treaties contain a provision known as a "saving clause." Exceptions specified in the saving clause may permit an exemption from tax to continue for certain types of income even after the recipient has otherwise become a U.S. resident alien for tax purposes.

If you are a U.S. resident alien who is relying on an exception contained in the saving clause of a tax treaty to claim an exemption from U.S. tax on certain types of income, you must attach a statement that specifies the following five items:

1. The treaty country. Generally, this must be the same treaty under which you claimed exemption from tax as a nonresident alien.

2. The treaty article addressing the income.

3. The article number (or location) in the tax treaty that contains the saving clause and its exceptions.

4. The type and amount of income that qualifies for the exemption from tax.

5. Sufficient facts to justify the exemption from tax under the terms of the treaty article.

Cat. No. 10231X

Form **W-9** (Rev. 1-2003)

PAYMENT

Most large counties require certified funds for buying liens. The problem, of course, is that you don't know how many liens you will actually get, or what the total dollar amount of those liens will be before the auction. In most cases, the county will give you a period of time to get the accurate amount of funds. That time is usually 2 to 24 hours. Here are a few examples:

- **District of Columbia.** The investor must always have at least 10 percent (of what you will buy) on deposit with the tax collector. If your purchasing balance drops the deposit below 10 percent, you will be asked to increase your deposit before continuing to purchase liens. You pay the balance in full at the end of your buying or the end of the sale.
- **Indianapolis, Indiana.** No deposit is required. The investor pays for the lien, in certified funds, as soon as he wins the bid. The county's treasurer sits up front, and the winning bidder makes his or her way there immediately to pay for the lien. Most investors will give the county a large cashier's check to cover their buying for the entire day.
- **Iowa.** No deposit is required. A few large counties will charge a small fee ($75 to $150) for a bidding card. Payment is made for the purchases at the end of the day in certified funds, although some small counties will allow personal checks.
- **Florida.** A $1,000 deposit is generally required in the larger counties. Some counties will mail an invoice to the investor about two weeks after the sale (with about two weeks to mail certified funds). Other counties will give the investor one or two days to return with certified funds. See Figure 4.3 for my examples from Orange and Seminole counties.

As you can see, every county sets its own rules for timely payment. Check with each county before the sale for its rules. Each county will have a "Tax Sale Guidelines" handout setting forth its rules and regulations. See Appendix A.

FIGURE 4.3 *Successful Auction Examples*

CERTIFICATE SALE BILLING

DATE: 06/02/2003

BUYER NO:

BIDDER NO: 81

NAME: NATIONAL TAX LIEN INSTITUTE

ADDRESS:

BALANCE DUE $33,237.07   20

LESS DEPOSIT   1,000.00

BALANCE DUE $32,237.07

PLEASE REMIT BY CASHIER'S CHECK, MONEY ORDER, OR CASH

TO: EARL K. WOOD, Orange County Tax Collector
     P. O. BOX 2551
     ORLANDO, FLORIDA 32802

PAYMENTS NOT RECEIVED IN THIS OFFICE BY JUNE 12, 2002
       WILL RESULT IN FORFEITURE OF DEPOSIT
              AND LOSS OF CERTIFICATES.

FOR FURTHER INFORMATION, PLEASE CALL:

BARBARA HOWE   -   (407)836-2708

EARL K. WOOD, TAX COLLECTOR
The Sun Trust Center Tower • 200 South Orange Avenue • Reply To: Post Office Box 2551 • Orlando, Florida 32802-2551
(407) 836-2705 • http://www.tax.co.orange.fl.us

FIGURE 4.3 *Successful Auction Examples (Continued)*

CERTIFICATE SALE BILLING

DATE: 06/02/2003

BUYER NO:

BIDDER NO: 71

NAME: LOFTIS LARRY

ADDRESS:

BALANCE DUE $12,429.32   14

LESS DEPOSIT   1,000.00

.BALANCE DUE $11,429.32

PLEASE REMIT BY CASHIER'S CHECK, MONEY ORDER, OR CASH

TO: EARL K. WOOD, Orange County Tax Collector
     P. O. BOX 2551
     ORLANDO, FLORIDA 32802

PAYMENTS NOT RECEIVED IN THIS OFFICE BY JUNE 12, 2002
     WILL RESULT IN FORFEITURE OF DEPOSIT
          AND LOSS OF CERTIFICATES.

FOR FURTHER INFORMATION, PLEASE CALL:

BARBARA HOWE - (407)836-2708

EARL K. WOOD, TAX COLLECTOR
The Sun Trust Center Tower • 200 South Orange Avenue • Reply To: Post Office Box 2551 • Orlando, Florida 32802-2551
(407) 836-2705 • http://www.tax.co.orange.fl.us

FIGURE 4.3 *Successful Auction Examples (Continued)*

RAY VALDES
SEMINOLE COUNTY TAX COLLECTOR

P. O. Box 630 • Sanford, Florida, 32772-0630 • 407-665-1000 • www. seminoletax.org

June 5, 2003

NATIONAL TAX LIEN INST.   (293)

Dear Tax Certificate Buyer:

Enclosed is a list of tax certificates we show purchased with your bidde number during the 2003 Tax Certificate Sale held May 28 thru May 30, 2003

Your purchase of ___50_ tax certificates amounts to ___$35,975.31_. Your deposits total ____$4,000.00_, leaving a balance due of ___$31,975.31_.

As a reminder, any certificate acquired by bid that had the taxes paid during the sale or prior to 5:00 pm Friday, May 30th, has been deleted.

In order to verify your successful certificate bids, paid tax parcels are on your list, but noted "Taxes Paid - No Certificate Issued", and the amount is not included in your balance due.

Your remaining purchase balance must be received in our Sanford office by June 12, 2003, and must be in the form of certified funds.

Our triple audit system has cross referenced, verified, and balanced ever item of the sale. If you have any questions, please contact this offic at (407) 665-7641.

Very truly yours,

Lynda J. Hedrick

Lynda J. Hedrick
Tax Manager

County Services Building	Wilshire Plaza	Oak Groves Shoppes	Oviedo City Hall
1101 E. First Street	384 Wilshire Blvd.	995 N SR 434	400 Alexandria Blvd.
Sanford, FL 32771	Casselberry, FL 32707	Altamonte Springs. FL 32714	Oviedo, FL 32765

LARRY'S REMINDERS

- Lien sales typically occur annually, while deed sales may occur biannually, quarterly, monthly, or even weekly.
- Most jurisdictions have only live auctions, but online auctions are becoming more popular with tax collectors.
- Typically, you are allowed only one bidder card per person in the auction room.
- To receive a bidder card, you will need a Social Security number or tax identification number. You can invest personally, or though an entity like a corporation, trust, or retirement account.
- Many counties will require a deposit before allowing you to bid. Review each county's rules prior to attending the auction.

5

BIDDING

Tricks of the Trade

*"What? You mean that I only get the interest rate on
the lien amount, not on the premium?"*
DISTRICT OF COLUMBIA INVESTOR ON THE *THIRD* AUCTION DAY

A few years ago, I attended a tax lien sale in Washington, D.C. I purchased some liens on the first day of the sale and then left to attend another sale the next day. The following day, the third day of the D.C. sale, I returned to D.C. to buy more liens. I arrived during a break, so only a few people were remaining in the room. While looking for a place to sit, I overheard a conversation going on behind me. A lady was discussing the sale rules with another investor. With a look of shock on her face she exclaimed, "What? You mean that I only get the interest rate on the lien amount, not on the premium?" I knew exactly what happened. This lady, who now had been buying liens for three days, just found out that she was not getting any interest on the premiums for her liens.

In D.C. and other jurisdictions, the investor bids a "premium" over the lien amount. The investor receives 18 percent on the lien, but no interest at all on the premium bid. For example, if the lien amount was $1,000 and I bid $2,000, my yield would be 9 percent, since I received 18 percent on the first $1,000 but no interest on the second $1,000. Suffice it to say, this poor lady's overall return was well below what she originally thought. The time for learning the rules for a tax lien sale is *before* the auction, not three days into it!

While bidding procedures are typically dictated by state law, most states give the county official who runs the sale (usually either the county treasurer or tax collector) great leeway in the matter. For example, a state statute might state that the official bidding method is "bid down the ownership," while the county official actually uses a "rotational" system. For that reason, an investor should always review the county's bidding rules and speak with a county official and other seasoned investors before bidding.

BIDDING SYSTEMS

States generally use one of the following five types of bidding systems.

Bid Down the Interest

A "bid down the interest" system means that the state sets a maximum rate, but bidders at the auction may bid a lower amount acceptable to them. For example, Florida is a "bid down the interest" state, starting at the statutory maximum of 18 percent. At Florida live auctions, each bidder will receive a placard with a bidder number on it. When the official announces a particular lien, the investors who want that lien raise their numbers and shout out the interest rates they will accept. The county official typically waits until the bidding stops and awards the lien to the lowest bidder. If no one offers a rate below the statutory rate but several bidders have raised their cards, the county official will sell the lien to one investor at 18 percent by picking the investor at random.

I have attended the Orlando tax lien sale regularly since 1999 and always seem to pick up interesting stories. In 2003, for example, a lady walked into the sale (it was not an online auction then) on the second day of a weeklong auction. I assumed it was her first auction, since she came late in the afternoon of the second day and walked directly to the front of the room to get a seat in the front row. In Orlando (and most cities), institutional investors send representatives at 6 AM (or earlier) to make sure they get seats in the first row, and these seats are always taken shortly after the doors open. Looking around for a while, she finally found a seat in the third row. What happened next will require a little background on the Orlando sale.

Since Florida is a very good lien state, a number of institutional bidders (e.g., Wachovia Bank, Bank Atlantic, and a couple of private funds) will bid at the auctions in the larger cities like Orlando, Miami, Fort Lauderdale, and Tampa. All of the auctions in Florida take place in May and June. Since Orlando is always the first auction in the state, these institutional bidders train their representatives, so that they can invest without supervision in the other cities. I normally see about four or five institutional bidders at this sale. These investors are very aggressive in bidding rates for several reasons:

1. They have millions of dollars to invest.
2. There are many beautiful properties on which to buy liens.
3. Florida has a minimum penalty of 5 percent (which means that even if you bid to 1 percent, if the owner redeems, he or she has to pay a minimum of 5 percent). For example, if I bid 1 percent and the owner redeems one month later, I get 5 percent, or a 60 percent rate of return ($5 \times 12 = 60$).
4. The institutional investors know that most of the nice properties will redeem quickly, triggering the 5 percent minimum.
5. If the owner does not redeem the lien and the investor forecloses on the lien by buying out the other lien (a two-year redemption period means two sales), the county gives the investor a new certificate for 18 percent, which accrues until the actual deed auction to sell the property and pay off the lien holder.
6. Based on numbers 3 to 5 above, these investors know that their total yield will far exceed what their bid amount was at the auction.

Given this information, the institutional bidders in Orlando recently have begun to bid most liens on nice properties down to $\frac{1}{4}$ percent, the minimum bid under Florida law. They do this by yelling "Quarter," which means one quarter of 1 percent. My estimate is that their overall yield will be in the range of 8 to 10 percent, if I average out their returns on all liens. Now back to our newcomer at the auction.

After watching the institutional investors bidding "quarter" on many large, expensive properties, this lady began to jump in, also bidding "quarter" very aggressively. It didn't make sense to me, or to the institutional investors sitting in front of me. If she was an institutional bidder, she would have been there on the first day, got a seat in the front row, and had very organized notebooks on the properties coming up (where investor representatives are shown which properties to bid on and to list for their company the percentage at which they bought a lien). After she had bought five or six liens at $\frac{1}{4}$ percent, the institutional investor in front of me surmised that these would all default, meaning that the investor wouldn't be able to pay for them and they would go back to the county. I agreed. She went on to buy several more liens before the day was over, covering properties valued at over $1 million.

At the beginning of the sale the next day, a county official made an announcement that we all expected. He said, "Folks, remember that you are bidding on the lien *percentage,* not the property itself." Translated: The lady yesterday bidding $\frac{1}{4}$ percent on all those properties thought she was *acquiring* those properties for one-quarter! As absurd as this sounds, it's a true story. She simply did not know the rules or what was going on.

But the story's not over! Later that day when this lady was bidding and buying liens at $\frac{1}{4}$ percent, she decided to change seats. She wanted to be in the seats where the institutional bidders were sitting. Directly in front of me were three representatives from one institutional bidder company. They were college students on summer break making some extra money working for this company at the auction. One of them, a young man probably 20 years of age, went out of the room for a break. Like most people, he left his bidding placard on his seat so that no one would take his spot while he was away. While he was outside, our aggressive newcomer lady decides she's going to take his seat in the second row. She does and begins bidding and buying again. After about 30 minutes, she sees a seat open up in the first row so she takes her belongings and moves again.

Shortly thereafter, the college student returns and takes his old seat. Since he's sitting directly in front of me, I see him begin to look around for something—under his seat, next to him, on the floor around him. He has a very worried, if not distraught, look on his face. I realized what had happened. The rookie lady who had taken his seat also had taken his bidding card with her to the new seat in the front row! I tapped the young man on the shoulder and explained that the lady had taken his seat while he was outside and that she might inadvertently have taken his number. I might as well have told him that he had cancer! Since everyone knew this lady was clueless, he knew of the danger of her having his bidding number. So he politely tapped the lady and asked, "Ma'am, you don't have my bidder card, do you?" She fumbled through her belongings and, finding it, said, "Oh, I'm sorry, I sure do; here you go." Horrified, the young student exclaimed, "You didn't buy anything with it, did you?" She didn't *think* so. So the second lesson from this story is to always have your bidding card with you or with a trusted associate!

Premium Bidding

Premium bidding occurs where the county awards the lien to the investor bidding the highest premium above the lien amount. For example, on a $500 lien, the winning bid may be $1,000: the $500 lien plus a $500 premium. What will differ, however, is how the county will treat the interest rate for the winning bid. Counties generally use one of the following five systems:

1. The premium and the lien both receive the same interest rate or penalty.
2. The premium and the lien both receive interest, but at different rates.
3. The lien amount receives interest, while the premium amount does not.
4. The premium amount receives interest, while the lien amount does not.
5. The premium is lost (the investor does not receive his principal back on any premium paid).

The example at the beginning of this chapter shows that the District of Columbia offers no interest on the premium portion (#3). In other areas, like Texas for example, the investor will receive his or her interest rate or penalty on both the lien amount and the premium (#1). This system is the best scenario for the investor, since the investor really does not care what the bidding goes to because he'll get his penalty or interest return on the entire amount.

Indiana uses system #2, paying a different rate for the premium and the lien. Indiana has a penalty return on the lien amount (10 percent or 15 percent, depending on the redemption date). However, any premium amount (which they call an "overbid") receives only 10 percent simple interest. While this tends to reduce your overall rate of return, a small overbid carrying 10 percent interest will not disappoint too many investors. One additional note about the Indiana system: in Indianapolis, the county official uses a PowerPoint system to list liens for sale on the screen (as do many counties). An unusual aspect of their sale, however, is that they list 25 liens at a time on the screen, and any interested bidders simply voice their interest in one of the liens. If others want to bid on the one you just announced, they do so by raising their bidder cards to acknowledge a premium bid. If no one else raises his or her card, you get it at the minimum bid.

In systems #2 through #5, prepared investors simply adjust their bids before bidding so that they get their acceptable rates of return. For example, if your jurisdiction pays no interest on your premium but pays 18 percent on the lien amount, someone who wants at least a 9 percent rate of return cannot bid more than $2,000 for a $1,000 lien. If you can acquire that lien for bidding only $1,500, so much the better, as you'll be getting a return of 12 percent.

Random Selection

In a random selection jurisdiction, the county official will randomly select a bidder number and ask that investor if he or she wants the particular lien up for sale. If that bidder declines, the official will select another bidder and once again ask if the bidder wants the lien. This process continues for several rounds. If none of the bidders selected wants the lien, the county official will typically ask, "Does anyone want this lien?" If anyone wants it, that bidder is awarded the lien.

The method used for random selection will depend on the number of bidders in attendance at the sale and the sophistication of the county administration. Several years ago, I was investing in Shelby, Iowa, a small but very quaint and friendly town. While Iowa is officially a "bid down the ownership" state, most of the counties use the random selection process. The day before the Shelby sale, I spoke with the county treasurer. She confirmed that Shelby was officially under the "bid down the ownership" system, but that I could "ask" for the random selection system publicly before the sale began the next day. I did, and naturally the other investors did not oppose the motion.

Since there were only 22 bidders at the Shelby County sale (actually about 10 if you consider families as one bidder), the county put 22 Ping-Pong balls in a large KFC bucket with a bidder's number on each ball. A county official then simply reached into the bucket, picked a ball, and announced the number of the bidder selected.

Since this method is not too scientific, one Ping-Pong ball near the top might get a larger number of liens. As I recall, bidder number 8 was chosen a disproportionate number of times, once in succession!

In a large county like Polk County (Des Moines), Iowa, the county employs a computer to randomly select bidder numbers. Under this method, the county simply displays the number selected on a large screen, together with the lien being sold. Once displayed, the investor simply announces whether he or she desires to purchase the lien. If he or she declines, the computer selects another bidder.

One other aspect of this bidding is worth mentioning. Some counties will switch to this system without notice if they get behind schedule. For example, Florida officially uses the "bid down" method. However, the county tax collector has only a few days to sell thousands of liens. If every lien is slowly bid down, this consumes valuable time. Say we have a lien that comes up and one bidder says 17 percent, the next says $16\frac{3}{4}$ percent, the next says $16\frac{1}{4}$ percent, then 16 percent, then $15\frac{3}{4}$ percent, and so on. If most of the liens are bid this way in the first day or two, the county will likely get behind schedule and not finish on time (often a problem since the auction hall for a large county will be rented). The county official in charge only has one option—to sell a lot of liens very quickly to catch up. How does the official do that? I've seen it many times. The official just takes the first bidder card he or she sees, or the first number that he or she hears. In essence, the official has just switched to a random selection system in order to catch up. I have found this switch to occur late in the day, since that is when the official gets an accounting of where he or she is in the overall sale. My advice to you: Stay until the very end every day! (Note: One reason that I dislike online bidding is that it eliminates this strategy.)

Rotational Bidding

When I bought liens in Woodbury County, Iowa, I found the rotational system very fair. Under this system, each investor receives the same number of chances to purchase a lien. Here, the county official simply looks at the list of liens, starts at the top, and asks bidder #1 if he or she wants the first lien on the list. If bidder #1 declines, bidder #2 is asked, and so on. Let's suppose that bidder #2 declines but bidder #3 takes the lien. Bidders #2 and #3 don't lose their "turn," however, since they were responding to the lien allocated to bidder #1. So, when the official gets a taker on the first lien, the next lien is offered to bidder #2.

This type of system is probably most fair, since bidders will get an equal number of opportunities to buy liens. But here's the downside—if on your turn you get a $150,000 lien that you cannot afford, too bad; you now have to wait another cycle for your turn again. The same holds true if on your turn you get a $190 lien on a vacant lot. The upside, of course, is that under this system, like the random selection system, everyone gets the same, maximum return. In the case of Iowa, that's a nice 2 percent per month, or 24 percent annual return.

Bid Down the Ownership

This system is the least desirable of all the systems, and both investors and county officials dislike it. Under the "bid down the ownership" system, investors bid down how much of the property the lien will encumber. For example, if there is no bidding, the lien is sold at face value, earns the statutory interest rate, and encumbers 100 percent of the property. However, a bidder may say he or she will buy the lien accepting an encumbrance on only 75 percent of the property, or 50 percent, or 25 percent, or even 1 percent! How crazy is this? How would an investor possibly enforce the lien or foreclose on it? In short, it would require a court order to sell the property and apportion the proceeds according to percent of ownership!

While Nebraska and Iowa both "officially" use this system, most counties try to avoid it. During my visit to Iowa for the 2001 sale, for example, I saw that Shelby, Monoma, Harrison, and Polk counties used the random selection bidding system, while Woodbury used the rotational bidding system.

Over-the-Counter

Over-the-counter is not an official bidding system. This method is used to buy liens after the sale occurs. For example, if the county has liens left over after a sale, an investor can come to the county and purchase any liens in "inventory." Literally, investors can buy liens over-the-counter at the tax official's office. I purchased a lien in Omaha, Nebraska, this way. Keep in mind that if you are buying over-the-counter, no one is bidding against you. As such, you will always get it at the statutory maximum rate (14 percent for my Nebraska lien). If the state you are thinking about has a very high interest rate, it is likely that all of the liens will be purchased at the sale. However, what most people forget is that a certain number of liens purchased at the sale will default. For example, an investor may have bought the lien thinking it was for another property, and the county allowed him or her to void the sale. That lien may not be offered for sale again at the auction. Likewise, an investor may have purchased 20 liens at the auction but failed to come up with the cash at the end of the sale (some counties will bill you). If so, the county will have to take those liens back as well. All of these defaulted liens will be returned to the county's "inventory" and typically can be purchased for the statutory maximum rate, after the sale, over-the-counter.

In Figure 5.1 you will see the Nebraska lien that I purchased over-the-counter. Notice at the top of the lien it states "Private Sale." That just indicates that the sale of this lien occurred privately (to me) and not at a public auction.

TRICKS OF THE TRADE

I'm often asked by new or prospective lien investors, "How can I compete with the institutional investors that are at the tax

FIGURE 5.1 *Nebraska Over-the-Counter Lien Purchase*

PRIVATE SALE 01-05612

COUNTY TREASURER'S CERTIFICATE OF TAX SALE

STATE OF NEBRASKA
COUNTY OF DOUGLAS   I, JULIE M. HANEY Treasurer of the County of Douglas, in the State of Nebraska, do hereby certify that the following described Real Estate in said County and State, to wit:

0139-5568-16

LAKE CUNNINGHAM HILLS   LOT   285   BLOCK   0
IRREG

was, on the 21ST DAY OF JUNE, A.D. 2001   duly sold by me in the manner provided by law at Private Sale at my office, for the Delinquent Taxes

99/00	$270.32 +	40.23 + 5.00 =	$315.55
WEEDS 1	$110.00 +	24.98 =	$134.98

amounting to   450.53   Dollars, including interest and penalty thereon, and the costs allowed by law, to LARRY B. LOFTIS
for the said sum of   460.53   Dollars. And I further certify that such Real Estate has been offered at public sale for taxes but not sold for want of bidders, and that unless redemption is made of said Real Estate in the manner provided by law, the said LARRY B. LOFTIS
heirs or assigns, will be entitled to a deed therefor on and after the 21ST DAY OF JUNE, A.D. 2004
on surrender of this Certificate and Compliance with the provisions of the Revenue Law.
    IN WITNESS WHEREOF, I have hereunto set my hand this 21ST DAY OF JUNE, A.D. 2001

COPY   *Julie M. Haney*

$460.53   100%   Treasurer of Douglas County, State of Nebraska.

sales?" The question, of course, makes several assumptions. First, it assumes that institutional investors are at this sale. Typically, institutional investors appear only at sales of large counties (a metropolitan area, say, with a population of over 500,000). Second, it assumes that you are bidding on the same properties as the institutional investors. In many cases, that competition may not occur. Many prospective investors also are intimidated by large crowds and assume they will not be able to get good rates of return. Let's look at some of the tricks of the trade that will assist you in getting the jump on the competition, or competing with institutional investors. These tips apply to the most common bidding system, "bid down the interest," or its variation of "bid up the premium." Obviously, these tips apply to live auctions rather than online sales.

Buy at Smaller Counties

Institutional investors typically have several million dollars to spend at a single tax lien sale. It would not make sense for them to attend a sale for a small county that only has, say, $750,000 in liens to sell. For example, in my county, Orange County, Florida, several institutional investors routinely purchase over $3 million of liens. Keep in mind, of course, that these large counties will have tens of thousands of liens to sell. To avoid competing against these bidders, just go to the counties where they will not be going—small counties. In most states with good rates, you will find two to four very large metropolitan areas where institutional investors likely will attend the sales. In Florida, these investors will invest in the Miami/Ft. Lauderdale area, the Tampa/St. Petersburg area, Orlando, and Jacksonville. But Florida has 67 counties. So, rule number one is to consider going to (or investing online, if available) a sale in a smaller city. I typically go to smaller counties to get higher yields (typically in the 10–15 percent range).

Buy Smaller Liens

Assume you decide to go to a sale (or bid online) in a large jurisdiction. How do you compete with institutional investors who are buying large numbers of liens at very low rates? Buy smaller liens. Most institutional investors only buy liens above a certain dollar threshold, typically between $1,000 and $1,500. In most cases, you can buy liens of $300 to $1,000 that are usually "below the radar" of these institutional bidders. In essence, you are trading off the quality of the property for a higher interest rate; that is, the house behind a $700 lien will not be nearly as nice as the house on a $2,000 lien. The numbers are relative, of course, since you are still looking at a lien that represents 1 to 2 percent of the fair market value of the property. If you buy a $300 lien, you're probably looking at a vacant lot. Again, it's the same adage, "Greater risk, greater reward." You'll get the best rates on those small liens, because they will be more likely not to redeem since no one lives on a vacant lot. I usually try to stay above about $450. If no institutional bidders are present, I try to stay above about $750.

Buy Liens on Nonhomestead Properties

Here's another tip to avoid competing with institutional bidders. Probably one-half of the institutional bidders (sometimes more) will not buy a lien on residential property that is not a "homestead" property. A homestead designation means that the property is someone's personal residence, and that person filed for the exemption with the county. In my estimation, maybe 25 percent of people who would qualify for a homestead exemption never do, for whatever reason. By filing for the exemption, the county deducts a certain number (in my state, $25,000) off of the county's appraised value of your home, thus lowering your property tax bill. Institutional bidders know that a homestead property has a higher likelihood of redemption because it is a personal residence. In addition, the designation assures the investor that the property is not a vacant lot. Because you can find out if the property is improved with the appraiser's office, I buy many liens that are not homesteads.

Stay during "Off" Times of the Sale (at Live Auctions)

What are "off" times of a sale? An off time is when most of the other bidders are not in the room. When is that? Lunchtime! The majority of counties will bid right through the lunch hour by just alternating county officials conducting the bidding process. Most of those in attendance have been in the sale room since early in the morning and are hungry! As such, they get a bite to eat from noon to 1 PM. What is another off time? After 5 PM! Most people are creatures of habit, and the workplace normally says that the day ends at 5 PM. Remember that institutional bidders do not have vice presidents at the sales. Rather, they hire college students or agents whom they may use every year. Most of these people have been at the sale since 8:30 AM and are ready to leave at 5 PM. Also, parents may leave around 4:30 PM to pick up a child from school or day care. Other investors are just worn out from sitting all day and leave around 5 PM. *Use these off times to your advantage!* Some of the best rates will occur then because there are few people in the room.

My favorite trick of the trade is to stay after the posted closing time of the sale. For example, the county may hand out a flyer that says the auction will run from 8:30 AM until 5:00 or 5:30 PM. When the clock hits the official closing time, however, the county official realizes that he or she is behind schedule to finish the sale in the set number of days. To solve this problem and catch up, the official announces then that the sale will continue until 6 PM or 7 PM. Most investors are long gone by then.

Another off time is the last day of the sale. Oftentimes, the county will only need a few hours in the morning of the last day to finish the sale. Since most bidders have been there for several days and have bought their fair share of liens (or, in the case of individual bidders, have run out of money!), they either do not show up on the last day or leave an hour or so before the end.

I recall being at a sale last year where I missed most of the first day and the mornings of most days. It was now the last day. Most days there were about 25 bidders in the room. This last day there were 15. Four or five institutional bidders were at the sale, and the rates for liens in the $400 to $1,000 range were about 10 to 14 percent. At about 11 AM, an amazing thing happened—all of the institutional bidders and most of the other bidders left. But the sale was not over! I looked around the room, and there were only three of us left! One of the other bidders was an attorney friend who buys liens for his own account and is a seasoned investor. We looked at each other, smiled, and the bidding continued with just the three of us.

Why did everyone leave? At 11 AM, the county had finished its published list of liens. This is the official list that appears in the newspaper. However, the county also had a new, unpublished list that did not make the formal published list. There were maybe 50 liens on this list. The institutional bidders left because they had not been authorized by their employers to buy any of these liens. Since their employers never saw this small list, the agents knew they could not buy them. I do not know why the other bidders left—perhaps they thought the sale was over, were not interested in these new liens, or had run out of money. It did not matter to the three of us left in the room. We all purchased the remaining liens at between 14 and 18 percent.

You may be wondering why the three of us didn't just alternate liens and not bid against each other so we could get 18 percent on each lien. While this "secret" procedure does sometimes occur in some small counties, it is illegal under most state statutes, including Florida where we were bidding. Two of the three of us bidding were attorneys, so we know better than to do this. I also just wanted to have some fun with my friend. We'd been bidding at these sales for years and usually told each other which counties were looking good ratewise. So the prankster in me wanted to play with him a little bit. When he opened the bid at 17 percent, for example, I responded with 16¾ percent, and so on. . . . We had fun seeing who would go the lowest, but kept most of the liens in the 16 to 18 percent range.

Don't Hesitate

Have you heard the adage, "He who hesitates, loses"? This could not be more true than in tax lien investing. Auctions move—very fast! If you are not prepared, you will miss a good property or make a mistake. I have bought liens (and deeds) at great rates because other bidders hesitated. I've also lost good liens because I hesitated!

Let me illustrate a typical auction flow in a "bid down" lien state. The county official announces the lien and dollar amount and waits. Someone will yell out the interest rate at which they will take the lien, followed by others who yell out consecutively smaller numbers. For example, one person yells "16 percent." Then you hear "15¾ . . . 15½ . . . 15¼," and so on. After hundreds or thousands of liens have been sold, the crowd expects a certain tempo for this bidding. Some wait for the institutional bidders to start the bidding. I was at a large sale once where the institutional bidders were bidding down almost all of the excellent properties (say, values of $100,000 or more) to 5 percent or under. The institutional bidders were scooping up so many properties that many of the individual bidders left. A friend of mine who is a seasoned bidder came into the room in the afternoon and sat down next to me. A few minutes after he came in, a lien for over $9,000 was announced. At this particular sale, the institutional bidders were bidding down comparable liens to ¼ percent. My friend yelled out "17 percent." There was a one-second pause before the county official announced his bidder number. The audience was stunned.

All liens over $1,500 had been bid down to 5 percent or below all day long. My friend just hit a home run! The crowd instinctively responded with "Wooooo."

Why did the institutional bidders ignore this big lien? The property was a gas station, and they were not allowed to bid on it. All of the other bidders had been lulled to sleep by the constant barrage of institutional bidders going down to very low rates very quickly. Most bids opened at 5 or 6 percent. Before any of the individual bidders (probably 95 percent of the room) could respond to my friend's bid, it was gone. Everyone just assumed the institutional bidders would bid it down. Believe me, 20 people in that room would have loved to bid on that lien.

Always remember that the county cannot wait for others to jump in. If there is a slight pause in bidding, too bad, it's gone. The county does this for two reasons. First, there are hundreds or thousands or tens of thousands of liens to process, so the pace of the auction must move quickly to finish. Second, it would not be fair if county officials sometimes paused just because they thought a lien should be bid down further. Furthermore, once they have announced a winning bidder, they will not go back. On many occasions I've heard someone say, "What was the bid?" Too bad, too late. I've also heard people offer a lower rate; however, since the county official had already awarded the lien to another person, it was too late. You snooze, you lose! The good news is that, if you are at the auction long enough, this process will also work in your favor. Just be alert and be patient!

Keep in mind that if you are attending your first auction, watch for a while. Learn the tempo. Watch how fast it moves. Not long ago, I was training someone to bid for me at an auction. He watched me for a while and then I told him, "OK, I'm going to circle the one here that I want you to get. Go down to as low as 14 percent." He said, "OK." I watched him as it came up. The county official announced the lien and someone jumped in at 16 percent! Then another at 15½. I nudged him, "Jump in!" He froze. Then another, "15 percent." Gone. Someone got it for 15 percent. So I told him,

"Jump into the fray when it gets going." I gave him another lien, and as soon as the bidding began at 16½ percent, he yelled, "14 percent!" Yes, he got it, but he jumped from 16½ to 14. I had to teach him to see where the opening bid comes in and go just below that. He eventually got the hang of it, but it takes a few runs to be comfortable with the timing, tempo, and process of yelling out bids. It's also fun and exhilarating . . . the chase of the hunt!

LARRY'S REMINDERS

- States generally use one of five bidding systems: 1) bid down the interest, 2) premium bidding, 3) random selection, 4) rotational bidding, 5) bid down the ownership.
- To get better rates, buy liens at smaller counties, buy smaller liens, buy liens on nonhomestead properties.
- All auctions move very quickly. The auctioneer or county official must sell an enormous number of liens in a relatively short period of time. *You must pay careful attention at all times or you will end up missing your lien altogether or bidding on the wrong lien!* I certainly have missed my fair share of liens and have bid on, and purchased, the wrong lien on more than one occasion! If this ever happens to you, see the person conducting the sale at the *first* break and let him or her know of your mistake. In my experience, the county official will almost always let you off the hook if you mention it at the first break. If you wait until the end of the day, you'll get off the hook about 50 percent of the time. If you wait until the next day, you'll almost always be stuck with that lien. As such, check every lien that you purchased in *your* records with the county's printout of what you bought *before* you leave for the day.
- Before investing in an auction, review carefully the county's registration and bidding rules. If the system is an online bidding method, review carefully how it works. See Appendix A for examples.

6

WHAT IF THEY DON'T PAY? FORECLOSING ON YOUR SECURED INVESTMENT

A property tax lien is one of the most secured investments you'll ever find. In fact, your property tax lien is in first position, even ahead of a bank's mortgage on the property. Typically, liens against a property are set in a priority order, depending on the date the lien was recorded at the courthouse. For example, a house may have a first mortgage held by a bank in the first position, a home equity loan mortgage in second position, a mechanic's lien for repairs in third position, and so on. However, a property tax lien almost always takes priority over all other liens. Why is that? In short, property tax liens pay for virtually all county services—police and fire protection, schools, libraries, local roads, and local official salaries. If counties can't collect property taxes, you would not be able to call 911 for emergency service.

Let's assume a property has a fair market value of $200,000. Let's also assume that the property has a first mortgage with a balance of $120,000, and a second mortgage from a home equity loan with a balance of $15,000. Assume also that the property taxes are $2,500 per year (typically, property taxes are 1 to 2 percent of the fair market value). In the event of a foreclosure by anyone, here's the lien priority, or payout order, once the foreclosure sale occurs:

1. County property taxes: $2,500 (plus interest if paid late)
2. First mortgage (ABC Bank): $120,000
3. Second mortgage (XYZ Bank): $15,000

Let's assume that ABC Bank forecloses on its loan because the loan is in default for nonpayment. Let's further assume that the property taxes are delinquent and that an investor buys that lien at a tax lien sale. At the bank's foreclosure auction, the property tax lien holder will be paid before the bank, simply because the tax lien has a higher priority.

Now let's change the scenario. Assume that the bank's loan is not in default, but the property taxes are delinquent and that lien is bought by an investor at the tax lien sale. Now let's assume that the redemption period is about to expire and the owner has not redeemed or paid off the tax lien. At this point, the bank will almost always come in and pay off that tax lien to protect its position. That is, the bank knows that if the lien holder forecloses on the tax lien, the bank's mortgage will be wiped out. Accordingly, the bank will pay off a $2,500 lien, with interest, to protect its $120,000 mortgage behind that lien. Since banks inherently know the security of property tax liens, some banks, like Wachovia and Bank Atlantic, regularly invest in them.

Here's another twist. What if the state in which you are buying liens has a two- or three-year redemption period? What happens to the other lien holder(s)? Assume you are in a state with a two-year redemption period. Using our earlier example, here's the priority at payout:

1. Tax lien from year one: $2,500 (plus interest)
2. Tax lien from year two: $2,500 (plus interest)
3. First mortgage (ABC Bank): $120,000
4. Second mortgage (XYZ Bank): $15,000

We know that the lien bought in year one will have a redemption period expire one year before the lien bought in year two. Assuming that neither the property owner nor the two banks pay off the property tax liens, what happens? When the redemption period of two years runs out on lien #1, that lien holder can foreclose on his or her lien. While redemption of the lien can and will wipe out the mortgages (except in New Mexico, which is a deed state and would not involve this scenario), a lien holder cannot wipe out another *property* tax lien. So, if lien holder #1 wants to proceed with a tax lien foreclosure, he or she must pay off tax lien holder #2 (with interest). Thus, a tax lien holder is always protected. Lien holder #2 will be paid his or her principal investment, plus the statutory interest or penalty. Lien holder #1 now will either acquire the property free of all liens or have the property sold at a tax deed sale and be paid for his redemption of lien #2, plus his or her original investment and interest, depending on the jurisdiction.

FORECLOSURE TYPES

Generally speaking, states use one of two types of tax lien foreclosures. In the first type, the lien holder will acquire the property free and clear. For the purpose of this analysis, I'll refer to these jurisdictions as "administrative filing" states. In the second type of state, the lien holder will force the sale of the property at a tax deed sale and be paid off (or acquire the property if no one bids past the lien holder's credit for monies owed). I'll refer to these types of jurisdictions as "tax deed sale" states. Let's look at each type in detail.

Administrative Filing States

In an administrative filing jurisdiction, a lien holder desiring to foreclose on his or her lien must do the following:

1. Wait until the redemption period runs.
2. Notify the county of his or her desire to foreclose, which

may include the requirement to:

- pay a small administrative fee to the county;
- fill out and sign some paperwork with the county;
- send a notice to the property owner; and/or
- publish a legal notice in the local newspaper.

3. Pay off any other *property tax liens,* if applicable, and, in some cases, any "weed" lien imposed by the county for mowing the property.

In essence, upon completing the administrative procedures outlined above, the foreclosing lien holder will acquire the property free and clear. This type of procedure is used by most lien states.

Tax Deed States

In another type of foreclosure system, the lien holder only forces a tax deed sale. Florida uses this type of system. Here, the lien holder must follow the steps outlined above, except that the county will handle all notices. The county will then set the property for a tax deed sale. In Florida, this sale will occur about four months or so after filing for the sale with the county.

At any time up until this sale, the property owner may come in to redeem, or pay off, all the liens and costs. If the property owner does not, the sale will occur on the specified date. At the sale, the lien holder will be given a credit for his or her first position lien, plus interest; the second lien (which he or she bought out), plus the interest paid to that person; and the filing fee, plus any other costs the county may have charged. If the bidding does not exceed this credit, that lien holder now owns the property free and clear. If the bidding does exceed his or her credit and the lien holder does not wish to bid, he or she will be paid the credit amount, and the winning bidder will get the property free and clear.

This brings up a second investment option. Some real estate investors do not invest in tax liens but go to tax deed sales to acquire properties. Investors at tax deed sales can generally acquire properties for much lower sales prices than at a mortgage fore-closure. Mortgage foreclosure properties generally sell for 60 to 85 cents on the dollar, while tax deed foreclosure properties generally sell for 10 to 65 cents on the dollar. As you would expect, vacant lots will sell near the lower end of that spectrum while nice properties will sell closer to the higher end of the spectrum.

You would be surprised by what shows up at these sales. Of course, there are many residential lots being auctioned but also a few houses. I was at a sale a few years ago where a large commercial lot, several acres in size, was being sold. The property was on the corner of a busy intersection in one of the fastest-growing areas of town. In short, it was a prime commercial location. The ironic part is that the property was the parking lot for a huge Walgreens store! How did Walgreens let that happen? I don't know, but I can speculate. My guess is that the lot was separately deeded to Walgreens. Perhaps it was a different owner who sold that portion of land to Walgreens. I presume that the financial person who paid the property tax bills for Walgreens was in the corporate headquarters, probably located in a different state. Maybe the bill for this property never made it to that person's desk. I do know that the taxes for the store itself were paid, just not for the parking lot.

The bidding was frenzied. Two parties went back and forth for what seemed like hours (more like ten minutes, really). As I recall, the property sold for over $700,000. Remember, this was a huge commercial lot in a prime area of town. Perhaps the winning bidder wanted to develop part of the lot. In any event, that winning bidder knew that he could hold Walgreens hostage, because that was the only parking available for the store. In all likelihood, the new property owner will offer Walgreens a lease renewal at a very high rent. What choices does Walgreens now have? Walgreens can now either pay the high lease rate or close a store in a prime location, which it had spent hundreds of thousands, if not millions, of dollars to develop. Now if Walgreens decides to close the store and sell the property, who would buy a big retail store that has no parking? Leverage is an amazing tool in negotiation.

LARRY'S REMINDERS

- A property tax lien is a priority lien and takes precedence over other types of liens (except in New Mexico and state liens in Arizona).
- If a state has a redemption period of two or more years (and two or more tax liens will be sold), the buyer of the first lien has priority over the others. To foreclose on the lien, this investor must pay off the other property tax lien holder(s). A property tax lien cannot be extinguished by another lien.
- States generally use one of two systems to process foreclosure of a tax lien:
  1. Administrative filing
  2. Tax deed auction

7

NOTHING IS RISK-FREE, BUT THIS IS AS CLOSE AS IT GETS

You've probably heard the expression "the greater the risk, the greater the reward." Generally, this is true. In tax liens, however, you can achieve very high rates of return for very little risk. The last chapter illustrated how a property tax lien has priority over all other liens, including even a bank's mortgage. Because of that safety, some banks invest in tax lien certificates. But we all know that everything has some level of risk. Even certificates of deposit, or CDs, carry some risk (since they won't keep up with inflation, I prefer to call them certificates of depreciation). They are insured by the FDIC up to $100,000. But what if the FDIC goes bankrupt? What if there is a run on banks? These are unlikely events, of course, but still possible. Just ask the people who lost millions in the savings and loan crisis a few years back. So what are the potential risks with a tax lien investment?

THE INTERNAL REVENUE SERVICE

People often ask me, "Isn't the IRS ahead of you?" That is, will the IRS have a higher priority than a property tax lien? The answer is "yes" and "no." Under federal law (Section 7425(d), USC Title 26, Internal Revenue Service Code), the IRS has 120 days from the date of a public auction of the property (e.g., deed sale) to "redeem" or "buy out" your position. If the IRS chooses to redeem the property, it must pay:

- The actual amount paid for the property by the purchaser (i.e., the lien amounts), plus interest at 6 percent per annum from the date of the sale.
- The expenses of the sale, including protection and maintenance of the property that exceed any income received from the property.

So, if you purchase a lien on a property that has an IRS lien on it, the IRS lien "rides" with the property during your statutory redemption period. If the owner of the property does not redeem and you foreclose on your lien by forcing a tax sale (where the property transfers to you), the IRS clock starts ticking from the date of the sale. If the IRS does not redeem you, their lien on the property is extinguished.

So is the IRS *ahead* of you in the order of priority? Not really. Your lien cannot be wiped out by an IRS lien; your lien is not really "junior" to the IRS lien. The IRS just has a short window of time within which they can buy out your position. Your only "risk," if you want to call it that, is just getting a lower interest rate.

Here's the reality of the IRS "risk." I have bought hundreds of liens, and I have yet to see an IRS lien attached to one of the properties on which I purchased a lien. While I have seen IRS liens on properties at *deed* sales, I simply choose not to bid on those properties (in most cases, they are flagged as having the IRS lien).

BANKRUPTCY OF THE PROPERTY OWNER

In my estimation, maybe one lien in 200 (or more) will involve a bankruptcy of the property owner. That is, between the time you buy the lien and the time the redemption period expires, the owner files for bankruptcy. What happens to your lien if the owner files for bankruptcy?

Under federal bankruptcy law, once a person files for bankruptcy, the assigned federal judge will "stay" or stop all pending claims against that person and bring all actions into the judge's jurisdiction. This stay order will apply to all liens against that person or that person's assets. As a lien holder on the bankrupt person's property, you will receive a notice from the bankruptcy court to confirm your lien. The judge will separate all creditors into secured and unsecured creditors. Since you have a lien on real property, you are a secured creditor. And since your lien is a first-position lien, you have the highest priority against that property. In most cases, the judge will allow your lien to continue in first position against the property, and you will be paid your principal and the interest due. As such, your legal rights have not been impaired, only delayed. It is possible, however, for the judge to order the sale of the property and pay all secured creditors only a percentage of their claims.

Having said that, you want to avoid this potential risk if at all possible. In one scenario, the judge may only ask you to fill out a form indicating what your lien is and the interest you are owed. However, if the debtor names all creditors in the petition, you will need to file an "answer" with the court setting forth your claim, which will require the services of an attorney. If your lien is very small, it may not be worthwhile to even pursue the claim.

What's the best way to avoid getting a lien on a property that may later be encumbered with a bankruptcy? Buy larger liens. In general, a property tax lien represents 1 to 2 percent of the fair market value of a property. Accordingly, if you buy a $400 lien, the property is worth $20,000 to $40,000. If you buy a $3,000 lien, the property is worth $150,000 to $300,000. Which homeowner do you think is more likely to file for bankruptcy? Your risk of the owner filing for bankruptcy is small; nevertheless, it is possible.

WORTHLESS LOTS THAT WILL NOT REDEEM

Buying liens on worthless lots is the biggest potential risk in tax lien investing. This risk is totally avoidable, however, so pay careful attention to this section. Counties (and cities, too, when they conduct sales) are ruthless in both lien and deed sales. They have one purpose and one purpose only in selling a lien or deed—to collect property taxes due. Ninety percent of tax collectors could care less about what that lien is on. Ten percent really do care and do not want you to buy a lien on a worthless lot. For that reason, many tax collectors will not sell liens under $100. Unfortunately, the 90 percent of ruthless tax collectors will gladly sell you a $500 lien on a worthless lot.

What is worthless property? Imagine a vacant lot that is 10 feet wide by 100 feet long. What can you do with that lot? Because it is so small, you cannot build on it. I have seen many of these types of properties sold at lien and deed sales—lots that are side yards to residential houses; lots that are basically a drainage ditch; lots that have very odd configurations; and lots next to a transformer. Got the point?

If you buy a lien on a property like this, the property owner is not likely to pay off the lien. So what if you foreclose and even get the property; what will you do with it? To whom will you sell the property? I have learned this lesson the hard way!

How do you avoid these liens? First, don't buy small liens. If you have a $200 lien, it is most likely a vacant lot. Sure, you can buy a $2,000 lien on vacant property, but you will be dealing with a large piece of property in all likelihood. Second, the safest bet to avoid buying liens on vacant lots is to physically inspect the property before the sale. However, because you may be buying many liens, may not know the liens on which you will win the bidding, or may not know the area, this option may be impractical.

Third, another safeguard is to buy liens only on properties that are listed as "homestead." This designation means that it is someone's principal residence. This assures you that it is a house and that someone lives there. If so, the chances of the lien being redeemed are extremely high. Some institutional investors will invest only in properties listed as homestead. I don't personally take this route, because I also like liens on houses that are not homestead properties, as well as commercial properties. However, many investors do take this precaution to give them the most security.

A fourth safe way to avoid vacant lots is to buy in an area that you know. For example, in my county and the surrounding counties, I can tell from the listing in the newspaper where the property is and what type of property it is. In my newspaper, for example, the lien listing may show that the property is listed in a very nice subdivision, a good commercial area, or on a desirable street. I can tell from the entry if it is a residential house or commercial building. By the same token, I also know what the bad areas are and what to stay away from. Don't get me wrong—buying a lien on a house is still a safe and good investment, even in bad areas, because the lien still represents only 1 to 2 percent of the fair market value. Nonetheless, if I have a choice, I'll go for liens on nicer properties in nicer areas.

Many times I will buy in areas that I do not know, which means I do not know good areas from bad ones or good streets from bad ones. What do I do in this case? I look for liens over $1,000 in size. I look for properties that are shown as homestead or have an obvious commercial address. For example, a listing may reveal that it is in the First State Commerce Center. The name tells me that it is commercial. I've also seen plenty of liens on properties owned by companies you may have heard of—Walt Disney World, McDonald's, BellSouth Mobility, and virtually every major bank. I've bought liens on properties owned by Chase Manhattan Bank and LaSalle National Bank. In short, liens on properties owned by major corporations are typically very safe liens.

When in an unfamiliar area, there's one other thing you can do: check out the property with the county appraiser's office. In most instances, this can be done online. Just get the Web site for the appraiser's office and go to the search engine for properties.

Normally, you can pull up a property by the owner's name, the street address, the lot and block number, or the parcel identification number. For example, Figure 7.1 shows the appraiser's information on a property on which I bought a lien a few years ago.

Notice that the county's page gives me a photo of the property (somewhat unusual), the square footage, year built, assessed value, and other helpful information. While very few counties will provide a photo of the property, almost all will give you the square feet, year built, and assessed value. Keep in mind that the county's assessed value is normally around 80 to 85 percent of the fair market value.

If you buy using these guidelines, you can easily avoid buying liens on vacant lots. That's the good news. Here's the bad news. Remember the axiom "the greater the risk, the greater the reward"? Which liens do you think will command the highest rates of interest in a bidding jurisdiction? That's right, the smallest liens. But that's OK, because there's something for everyone. The institutional buyers like the big liens on the big properties and may bid them down very low, because the risk is almost zero. Likewise, many small investors prefer to invest in small liens for two reasons:

1. They can buy small liens that are affordable.
2. They can get the best rates of return.

EARLY REDEMPTION WITHOUT PENALTY

One downside of tax lien investing is that a lien may redeem very quickly, and the jurisdiction may not have a penalty for early redemption. Here's what I mean. Let's say you buy a lien at 12 percent interest. This means that it is 12 percent *per annum*. That's a nice rate of return, but what if it redeems after just one month? Yes, you will get a 12 percent return, but the dollar amount you receive will only be 1 percent of your principal. Now you will have to find another investment vehicle in which to park your money.

FIGURE 7.1 *Appraiser's Information on Lien Property*

Parcel Appraisal Summary - 832916000003

Page 1 of 1

Parcel Appraisal Summary - Shelby County Assessor

Shelby County, IA

Reference Number: 832916000003
Contract Holder: NEUMAN, DAVID B & GAIL A, SURV
BOX 135, ROUTE 1
SHELBY, IA 51570
Property Address: 700 BORDER ST
Legal Description: 33-78-40 PT NW SW

Class: R - RESIDENTIAL
School District: SHELBY-TENNANT COMM

Residential Dwelling

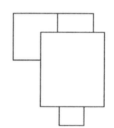

Sketch (click to enlarge)

Lot Area:	1.89 Acres; 82,161 SF
Occupancy:	Single-Family / Owner Occupied
Style:	2 Story Frame
Year Built:	1920
Exterior Material:	Aluminum/Vinyl
Above-Grade Living Area:	1,920 SF
Attic:	None
Number Rooms:	12
Number Bedrooms:	0
Basement Area Type:	Full
Basement Finished Area:	0 SF
Number of Baths:	2 Full Baths
Central Air:	No
Number of Fireplaces:	None
Garage:	220 SF - Det Frame (Built 1920)
Porches and Decks:	Wood Deck-Med (296 SF); 1 S Fr Opn (88 SF)
Yard Extras:	SHEDS; CATTLE SHED 13 X 35

Values		Sales			
	2000 Assessment	Date 1/17/1996	$ Amount $0	Sale Type (NUTC) 038	
Land:	$21,035				
Buildings:	$0				
Ag Dwelling or M&E:	$41,489				
Total:	$62,524				

Disclaimer: *The information in this web site represents current data from a working file which is updated continuously. Information is believed reliable, but its accuracy cannot be guaranteed.*

Because of that disincentive, many states include a penalty, either on top of a per annum rate or in lieu of an annual rate. Let's consider an example of two states.

Assume you purchased a $1,000 lien in Iowa. This state has a very nice interest rate of 2 percent per month. That's an annual fixed return of 24 percent, right? Now let's assume that you purchased another $1,000 lien in Florida at 6 percent. If both liens redeem after one year, what do you have? In Iowa, you made $240 for a 24 percent return. In Florida, you made only $60, for a 6 percent return. But what if both liens redeemed after only one month? In Iowa, you would have made 2 percent, or only $20. In Florida, however, you would have made $50, or a 60 percent *yield* because Florida has a minimum penalty of 5 percent. This penalty is just a small reward that Florida adds to make it a little more worth your while to invest there.

So, early redemption is not really a "risk" in tax lien investing. Rather, early redemption is just the downside of this type of investing. You still get a nice rate of return; however, you didn't make a lot of money in just one month and now you need to reinvest that money.

LARRY'S REMINDERS

- Property tax liens do not wipe out IRS liens, and vice versa. However, once a tax lien holder forecloses on his or her lien, if the IRS has a lien on the underlying property, the IRS will have 120 days from the date of the foreclosure sale to redeem and pay off the tax lien holder his or her principal, 6 percent interest, and all costs. After 120 days, the IRS lien will be extinguished from the property.
- If a property owner files for bankruptcy while a tax lien is outstanding (i.e., during the redemption period), a bankruptcy judge will stay all actions against the debtor and notify all creditors, including the tax lien holder. Depending

on the action taken by the debtor, the lien holder will need to either file an informal form with the bankruptcy judge (supplied by the court), or file a formal answer.

- Avoid buying liens on vacant lots, unless you have seen the property and know that it is buildable or salable.
- To diminish your risk, buy larger liens and liens designated as "homestead."
- For additional information on a property, go to the county appraiser's Web site. You normally can retrieve valuable information on a property by searching by parcel identification number or street address.

INVESTING IN TAX DEEDS

8

ATTENTION ALL
REAL ESTATE SCAVENGERS!

About one-half of the states are tax lien states, and the other half are tax deed states. Recall that I categorize ten states as "hybrid" states (see Chapter 1). These states, like Texas and Georgia, are deed states, but they have many aspects in common with lien states and operate much like a lien state.

We know that a tax lien state is one where a lien is filed on a property by the local jurisdiction for failure to pay the property taxes. The investor who buys that lien does not own the property. Rather, that investor only has a lien on the property. The investor is waiting for the owner to pay the taxes due, with interest or penalty, so that the investor can receive a nice rate of return on the investment.

A tax deed, however, is very different. If you buy a tax deed at a sale, you *own* the property from that day forward. With the exception of Arizona (which does not extinguish a prior state lien) and New Mexico (which does not extinguish any liens), and possible local special assessments, you own the property free and clear of other liens (save a county's mowing or "weed" lien to reimburse the county for mowing it, or in extreme cases, a demoli-tion lien). You can now do what you want with this property—rent it, resell it, or even live in it. In the normal tax deed state—what I will call a "pure" tax deed state—the owner has no chance to redeem. Keep in mind that the tax sale was no surprise to the owner. In most in-stances, that owner had notices and warnings from the county for years. So if you buy a tax deed, you own the property.

HYBRID DEED STATES

In hybrid states, however, the previous property owner still has a chance to redeem. Notice that I said "previous" owner. You own the property; however, the previous owner has a right to redeem for six months to two years, depending on the state and the type of property involved. For example, in Texas, if the property is nonag-ricultural and nonhomestead, the prior owner has just six months to redeem. If the property is agricultural or homestead, the prior owner has two years to redeem.

Keep in mind what the prior owner must do to redeem. First, he must come up with all of the back taxes, which he could not pay in the first place. Second, he must pay you off on any premium you may have paid at the sale. Third, he now has to come up with your penalty rate, which covers not only the lien itself, but your "overbid," plus county administrative costs.

In our Texas example, let's say we have a $200,000 piece of property. Let's also assume that the taxes are $3,000 per year. As-sume also that the owner is two years behind at the time of the sale, or $6,000 in arrears. In most cases, the bidding starts at the back taxes, or $6,000 (which typically also includes the county's administrative costs in bringing the sale, omitted for this exam-ple). Now let's assume that you paid $60,000 for the property at the sale, or $54,000 over the back taxes. If the prior owner is to redeem, he or she must now pay the $6,000 in taxes, plus your $54,000 overbid, plus county administrative costs, plus a 25 per-cent penalty on top of everything! What is the likelihood of that?

If the property is not agricultural or homestead, he or she would also have to come up with this amount in six months, since that's the redemption period for this type of property!

Yes, if the prior owner finds a lost rich uncle, he or she could possibly redeem. Are you crying about it? With a 25 percent penalty (a 50 percent rate of return at the worst, if it's nonagricultural and nonhomestead property) on your investment, you're not losing any sleep. In fact, you could have rented out the property during the months that you owned it, thus increasing your yield even more. But since the prior owner has this redemption right, however unlikely, you probably wouldn't want to put a new roof on a house. But there's nothing wrong with adding a few coats of paint and renting the place out while the redemption period runs.

STATES WITH BOTH LIEN AND DEED SALES

Florida is a lien state but also has monthly deed sales due to its foreclosure system. Ohio is a deed state but counties with populations over 200,000 are also allowed to have lien sales. New York is a deed state, but New York City is also allowed to have lien sales. Note again the breakdown of categories in Figure 8.1.

Investing in tax deeds, or properties, carries far more risk than investing in a lien on the property. But what generally comes with more risk? More reward! Assuming that you can buy the property at the right price, you can make a phenomenal rate of return on your money. What is the right price? The answer depends on what type of property it is, and what it will cost to put the property in prime resale condition. The answer also depends on how much money you have to invest. You may be able to get a $300,000 property for $50,000, but if you cannot come up with $50,000 for the auction, it doesn't matter what the property is worth. That's the first downside to this type of investing; it generally takes a considerable amount of money to get into the game. In the following chapters, we'll take a look at what kind of properties you can find, and just how much money you'll need to have a decent shot at getting them.

FIGURE 8.1 *State-by-State Categorization*

Lien	Deed	Hybrid
Alabama	Alaska	Connecticut
Arizona	Arkansas	Delaware
Colorado	California	Georgia
District of Columbia	Idaho	Hawaii
Florida[1]	Kansas	Louisiana
Illinois	Maine	Massachusetts
Indiana	Michigan	Pennsylvania[4]
Iowa	Minnesota	Rhode Island[5]
Kentucky	Nevada	Tennessee
Maryland	New Hampshire	Texas
Mississippi	New Mexico	
Missouri	New York[2]	
Montana	North Carolina	
Nebraska	Ohio[3]	
New Jersey	Oregon	
North Dakota	Pennsylvania[4]	
Ohio[3]	Utah	
Oklahoma	Virginia	
South Carolina	Washington	
South Dakota[6]	Wisconsin	
Vermont		
West Virginia		
Wyoming		

[1]Florida is a lien state but also has tax deed sales.
[2]New York City also is allowed to conduct tax lien sales.
[3]Ohio is historically a deed state; however, counties with populations over 200,000 also are allowed to conduct lien sales.
[4]Pennsylvania counties may operate under the hybrid system where the property is improved and has been legally occupied 90 days prior to the sale.
[5]For changes to Rhode Island laws, see the List of States section.
[6]As of July 1, 2006, South Dakota counties may no longer sell liens.

LARRY'S REMINDERS

- While a tax lien is only a lien on property, a tax deed conveys *ownership* of the property.
- A hybrid state is a deed state that operates like a lien state. While ownership of the property is conveyed, the prior

property owner still has a period of time to redeem the property.

- In almost all cases, a property acquired through a tax deed sale will be acquired free and clear of all liens (save a possible "weed" lien or demolition lien).
- See Part Three for a detailed list of states.

9

LOTS, DITCHES, AND A FEW GEMS

Over the years, I've seen a fair amount of hype in seminars and on television about getting nice properties for "pennies on the dollar." When I first got into tax lien investing, I thought this scenario would be quite common. After years of buying liens and deeds around the country, however, I've seen that getting a nice property for pennies on the dollar is quite rare. In most cases, properties sold at tax deed auctions are not "nice" properties. Makes sense, right? Why would someone lose a nice property at a tax deed sale?

At most tax deed sales, you will find many vacant lots, including a number of worthless lots, containing irregular or small parcels. In many cases, the county will readily sell you a drainage ditch. Because of this, it's always imperative for the investor to actually see the property before bidding. You will also see a few houses and even some commercial properties. The houses that I've seen at deed sales are typically vacant, often boarded up, and usually in disrepair. Investors at these sales buy such properties knowing that they will require a fair amount of rehabilitation. I've also bid on a few gems. While in Texas, for example, I bid on a set of seven condominiums. While I did see the outside of the complex, I could not get into the units. As such, I kept my bidding conservative and was outbid by another investor.

In Figure 9.1, you'll see a commercial building in New York that I bid on. Each section of the building was separately deeded. It was in a nice commercial area and across the street from a McDonald's restaurant. I was outbid there as well.

In my estimation, most deed properties sell at auctions for around 50 cents on the dollar. Oftentimes, however, it sells for more or less, depending on the quality of the property and the number of bidders present. In Figure 9.2, you'll see a property that I purchased in Kansas for only $4,100. The purchase price was in the area of about 8 cents on the dollar (given the sales prices in the neighborhood), but the property needed a lot of

FIGURE 9.1 *Commercial Building on Which I Was Outbid*

FIGURE 9.2 *A Safe Investment in Kansas*

work. Nevertheless, it was a safe investment. Figure 9.3 shows the Sheriff's Deed awarded.

At the same sale, I also purchased a couple of vacant lots. These were residential lots in decent areas, but the lots were very small. One lot required a variance from the building code, since it was five feet smaller than the code would allow for building. Since I bought these for only $75 each, these were also very safe investments. See Figures 9.4 and 9.5.

LARRY'S REMINDERS

- Most properties sold at tax deed sales will be vacant lots. Many of these lots will be worthless properties. However, a few nice properties may also be sold at a tax deed sale.
- Keep in mind that tax deed properties are sold for cash, and almost always will require rehabilitation.

FIGURE 9.3 *Example of Sheriff's Deed*

SHERIFF'S DEED

KNOW ALL MEN BY THESE PRESENTS, THAT a certain action to foreclose tax liens on certain real property in the County of Leavenworth, State of Kansas, has heretofore been filed in the District Court of Leavenworth County, Kansas, and is titled: The Board of County Commissioners of Leavenworth County, Kansas v. JL Clark Plumbing & Heating, Inc, et al, Case No. 0107 CV 224; and Judgement was thereafter rendered by said court in the above entitled action on 19 October, 2001.

In compliance with, and pursuant to this Judgment, the Clerk of the District Court of Leavenworth County, Kansas, issued an order to Sheriff Herbert F. Nye, Sheriff of Leavenworth County, Kansas, to advertise and sell tracts of land, lots, or pieces of real estate described below, all according to law.

The Leavenworth County Sheriff gave notice of this sale by advertisement and publication notice of sale in The Tonganoxie Mirror newspaper printed in Leavenworth County, Kansas, and which had been continuously and uninterruptedly published in Leavenworth County, Kansas, not less than fifty (50) weeks for a period of five years prior to the first publication notice, all according to the law. The Leavenworth County Sheriff, Herbert F. Nye, thereafter sold to Larry Boyd Loftis for the highest and best bid obtainable on 11 December, 2001, the following described real property; for the amount shown by each particular tract, lot, or piece of real estate.

DESCRIPTION: The South Half of Lot 26, and all of Lots 27 and 28 in Block numbered 33, Macaulay's First Addition to the City of Leavenworth according to the recorded plat thereof.

Price: $4,100.00

THEREAFTER, on the 17th day of December, 2001, the order of sale and the proceedings of sale were returned to the Leavenworth County District Court and after examination of the proceedings, and finding that the sale was made in all respects in conformity with the law applicable, the District Court of Leavenworth County confirmed the sale, and the proceedings made thereto, on the 18th day of December, 2001.

THEREAFTER, and according to law, the Sheriff of Leavenworth County was ordered to execute this good and sufficient deed to the purchaser(s) Larry Boyd Loftis.

I, Herbert F. Nye, Sheriff of Leavenworth County, Kansas, therefore do hereby give, grant, sell and convey to Larry Boyd Loftis, their heirs and assigns, forever, all the above-described real estate located in Leavenworth County, Kansas, together with all and singular tenements, hereditaments and appurtenances thereto or in any way appertaining, subject to zoning regulations, easements, restrictions, and mineral interests of record.

TO HAVE AND TO HOLD THE SAME UNTO THE SAID Larry Boyd Loftis, their heirs and assigns forever.

IN WITNESS WHEREOF, I, Herbert F. Nye, Sheriff of Leavenworth County, State of Kansas, have hereunto set my hand this 18th day of December, 2001.

Herbert F. Nye
Sheriff of Leavenworth County, Kansas

STATE OF KANSAS   )
)   SS:
COUNTY OF LEAVENWORTH   )

This instrument was acknowledged before me the 18th day of December, 2001 by Herbert F. Nye as Sheriff of Leavenworth County, Kansas.

K. Janette Nessmith - Eyerly
Notary Public - State of Kansas
My Appt. Expires 01-24-2004

Notary Public

My Appointment Expires:
01-24-2004

FIGURE 9.4 *Vacant Lot Purchased for $75*

FIGURE 9.5 *Example of Sheriff's Deed*

CORRECTED **SHERIFF'S DEED**

KNOW ALL MEN BY THESE PRESENTS, THAT a certain action to foreclose tax liens on certain real property in the County of Leavenworth, State of Kansas, has heretofore been filed in the District Court of Leavenworth County, Kansas, and is titled: The Board of County Commissioners of Leavenworth County, Kansas v. JL Clark Plumbing & Heating, Inc, et al, Case No. 0107 CV 224; and Judgement was thereafter rendered by said court in the above entitled action on 19 October, 2001.

In compliance with, and pursuant to this Judgment, the Clerk of the District Court of Leavenworth County, Kansas, issued an order to Sheriff Herbert F. Nye, Sheriff of Leavenworth County, Kansas, to advertise and sell tracts of land, lots, or pieces of real estate described below, all according to law.

The Leavenworth County Sheriff gave notice of this sale by advertisement and publication notice of sale in The Tonganoxie Mirror newspaper printed in Leavenworth County, Kansas, and which had been continuously and uninterruptedly published in Leavenworth County, Kansas, not less than fifty (50) weeks for a period of five years prior to the first publication notice, all according to the law. The Leavenworth County Sheriff, Herbert F. Nye, thereafter sold to Larry Boyd Loftis for the highest and best bid obtainable on 11 December, 2001, the following described real property; for the amount shown by each particular tract, lot, or piece of real estate.

DESCRIPTION: Lots 14 and 15, Block 101, Day and Macaulay's Subdivision, City of Leavenworth, Leavenworth County, Kansas.

Price: $75.00

THEREAFTER, on the 17thday of December, 2001, the order of sale and the proceedings of sale were returned to the Leavenworth County District Court and after examination of the proceedings, and finding that the sale was made in all respects in conformity with the law applicable, the District Court of Leavenworth County confirmed the sale, and the proceedings made thereto, on the 18th day of December, 2001.

THEREAFTER, and according to law, the Sheriff of Leavenworth County was ordered to execute this good and sufficient deed to the purchaser(s) Larry Boyd Loftis.

I, Herbert F. Nye, Sheriff of Leavenworth County, Kansas, therefore do hereby give, grant, sell and convey to Larry Boyd Loftis, their heirs and assigns, forever, all the above-described real estate located in Leavenworth County, Kansas, together with all and singular tenements, hereditaments and appurtenances thereto or in any way appertaining, subject to zoning regulations, easements, restrictions, and mineral interests of record.

TO HAVE AND TO HOLD THE SAME UNTO THE SAID Larry Boyd Loftis, their heirs and assigns forever.

IN WITNESS WHEREOF, I, Herbert F. Nye, Sheriff of Leavenworth County, State of Kansas, have hereunto set my hand this 3rd day of January, 2002.

            Herbert F. Nye
            Sheriff of Leavenworth County, Kansas

STATE OF KANSAS   )
)   SS:
COUNTY OF LEAVENWORTH   )

     This instrument was acknowledged before me the 3rd day of December, 2001 by Herbert F. Nye as Sheriff of Leavenworth County, Kansas.

     K. Janette Nessmith - Eyerly
     Notary Public - State of Kansas
     My Appt. Expires 01-24-2004

                               Notary Public

My Appointment Expires:

10

PENNIES ON THE DOLLAR?

Seminar speakers often suggest the possibility of buying a property for pennies on the dollar in tax deed or lien investing, as if anyone could do it at any sale on any type of property. Is it possible? Yes, I've done it. Is it common? No. As I mentioned in Chapter 9, most tax deed sale properties generally sell for around 50 cents on the dollar, in my experience. However, some areas are better than others; some auctions have fewer investors than others; and there are a few things that will increase your odds of getting a property extremely cheaply. Let's look at a few ways to really steal a property.

FORECLOSURE OF A TAX LIEN

The best way to acquire a property for pennies on the dollar is not to buy it at a tax deed sale—but at a tax lien sale. Here's why. At a tax deed sale, you will be competing with other bidders. Many of these bidders may be willing to buy it for 50 cents on the dollar, sometimes even more. If you purchased a lien at a tax lien sale, however, you are really buying for a rate of return. However, if the lien does not redeem, you may get the property for little more than one or two years of back property taxes.

While this situation is very rare, it does happen. In most lien states, the foreclosure process does not involve a public sale of the property but only a statutory requirement to send certified letters to the owner and lien holders—and typically a notice in the legal section of the local newspaper. In most cases, a foreclosing property tax lien holder is only paying off a subsequent property tax lien holder (if applicable), paying the back taxes, and reimbursing the county for its administrative fees for publication. In almost all cases, you should be wiping out any other liens. In short, you will be acquiring the property for pennies on the dollar. The downside, of course, is that you have to wait one, two, or even three years for the redemption period to run and to process the administrative foreclosure process with the county.

Is this scenario likely to happen on a nice property? No. First, what owner would let a property go like that? Second, if there is a mortgagee on the property, such as a bank, that mortgagee would step in and pay off the property tax liens to protect their position. In most cases, the owner will be either out-of-state, an entity such as a corporation or trust, or perhaps an heir who inherited the property but did not want it.

A few years ago I bid on an intercoastal property in Merritt Island, Florida. It was a normal house that needed some rehab, but was on a huge lot right on the intercoastal river. Most of the neigh-bors had nice sailboats moored at their docks. When I looked in the county's file on this property, I figured out what likely had happened. First, I saw that the owner, who was a woman, was liv-ing in the Northeast—Maryland as I recall. When I dug deeper in the file, I found a divorce decree. Apparently, many years before, the husband and wife had purchased this property as a winter home. My guess is that they likely had a nice sailboat or power-boat at their dock. While I didn't read the entire divorce decree (and the distribution of assets would not have been in this file), I assumed that the wife got this winter home as part of the settle-ment. However, since it was far away and she would be traveling alone, this waterfront property was not nearly as much fun as it used to be. In addition, perhaps the husband received the boat in the asset distribution. In any event, it appeared that the wife just didn't want it any longer and didn't want to continue paying the property taxes. Why not just sell the property? Your guess is as good as mine. Perhaps she was independently wealthy and elderly, or perhaps the house brought back too many bad memories. For whatever reason, the taxes were not paid and the county sold it at a deed auction.

In addition, the property did not have a mortgage. If it did, the mortgagee would have stepped in, paid the taxes, and then foreclosed on the mortgage. So, as a second requirement to stealing a property, you need to buy a lien on a property that is not encumbered by a mortgage or trust deed.

BUYING VACANT LOTS

The best deals at tax deed sales are almost always on vacant lots. It's common sense really. Would you lose a house for back taxes? Would you lose a commercial property? You might lose a lot if you were in some financial trouble and couldn't pay taxes due from two or more years. This asset is certainly less important.

As mentioned previously, many of these lots are of questionable quality or value. To be sure, though, you can buy them for pennies on the dollar—at least to the tax-assessed dollar value. I've bought them for as little as $75. I've also spent as much as $900 for a vacant residential lot. However, that lot was assessed by the county at $16,000 when I bought it, and was assessed at $20,000 the next year.

Does this mean that the property is worth $20,000? Not necessarily. While the tax-assessed value is typically in the range of 85 percent of the true fair market value, vacant lots are much harder to value. In some cases, they are completely worthless. I flipped the lot that I bought in Los Angeles for $900 to a land bank investor for $5,000 (he mailed me a postcard!). A friend of mine, however, bought a similar lot for $900 but did not receive a similar solicitation. It may be worth $10,000 or $20,000, or it may be worthless.

I live in Orlando, home of the world-famous Walt Disney World. This resort is the number one tourist destination in the world. The Disney property is larger than most counties and occupies thousands of acres. Growing up in Orlando, I know well the history of the development. Walt Disney and his team worked in great secrecy in the late 1960s to purchase hundreds of small acre lots to piece together the thousands of acres necessary for the development of Disney World. At the time, this land was very obscure and close to nothing. Today, the land is priceless. So who knows, maybe Disney will rebuild Disneyland in Los Angeles in the area where my friend holds her lot!

HANDYMAN SPECIALS

The third way to get great deals is to look at houses or properties that need much work. As you might expect, if a property is going to be sold at a tax deed sale, it needs a lot of work! Since I'm not particularly handy, I don't really like these properties. Yes, you can hire workers to do what is necessary, but you will reduce your profit and increase your out-of-pocket costs.

In the last chapter, I mentioned the house I bought for $4,100. I debated whether to get it for two reasons: One, it was in Kansas and I live in Florida. If I am an out-of-state owner, can you imagine the trouble I will encounter rehabbing the property? Second, the house needed a lot of work, and I didn't have time to get estimates from a general contractor. The prices in the area were around $50,000 (a very rural area), so I knew it was a safe investment. I was back in Florida the day after I bought it. In fact, I was very busy at the time and didn't have time to fool around with rehabbing or even thinking about it.

After sitting on it for a few months, I decided to put an ad in the paper to flip it for a few thousand more than I had paid, which I did. Had I been local to the property, I would have hired a general contractor and made much more. Nevertheless, it was a nice return on investment and represented only a few hours of work.

COUNTY MINIMUM BIDS

One last note to increase your odds of stealing a property. Most deed jurisdictions will open the bidding at the outstanding back taxes and county administrative costs. A few jurisdictions will have a higher amount. For example, if the property is a homestead residential property, some counties will require that bidding start at 50 percent of the tax-assessed value (maybe 35 to 40 percent of the fair market value). However, other counties allow opening bids *below* the outstanding back taxes. For example, when I was in Kansas, the county where I bought properties allowed for opening bids of only 50 cents!

Keep in mind that other bidders will be there but sometimes bidders run out of money. Sometimes, they are there to buy the property next to their own property and leave once that property is sold. In any event, all things considered, your preference would be to bid where the county has low opening bids.

In the list of states in Part Three, I give a few personal notes related to opening bids in a few states. There you will also find all pertinent information regarding bidding at sales for each state.

LARRY'S REMINDERS

- The best deals on acquiring properties is not on tax deeds, but on tax liens where the redemption period has expired.

- At tax deed sales, the best deals will usually occur on vacant lots, since fewer bidders will be interested in acquiring them.
- Be wary of tax-assessed values on vacant lots, because those figures may not be indicative of the lot's true fair market value.
- If you seek to acquire a property at a tax deed auction, you may want to invest in counties that have low minimum bids.

11

CAVEAT EMPTOR! RISKS AND HOW TO AVOID THEM

In the last chapter, I mentioned that many properties can be bought for very low prices, perhaps for even pennies on the dollar. However, many properties are not worth buying! For example, you might buy a vacant lot that is so small it is unbuildable. Or the lot is configured in such a strange way that it is also unbuildable, except possibly for use as a parking lot. In other cases, the property might be under water or next to or part of a drainage ditch! So, in tax deed investing, rule number one is always to personally view the property. Put your own two feet on the property being sold. Let's examine further this potential risk.

BAD PROPERTIES

When it comes to property taxes, counties have a double standard. On the one hand, the county insists that you pay property taxes each year. Those taxes are based on someone else's appraisal or assessed value (the county assessor). Oftentimes, that tax-assessed value may be way out of line with reality. I've seen drainage ditches assessed at $20,000! And what can you do about it? Nothing. Oh sure, you could challenge a tax assessor's valuation, but that requires some of your time finding out how to challenge it, arguing your case, and so on. On top of that, the assessor may just say that you are wrong and extract a tax from you for whatever he or she thinks is appropriate. In most cases, the assessor has never been to or even seen the property. The assessor is usually only looking at the historic records of what it has been assessed for and just adjusting for inflation.

A few years back, I was at a deed sale in Pennsylvania. I looked at a few properties before the sale. One of the properties listed by the county was a condominium in a very nice complex. Going by my rule to always personally see the property, I drove over to take a look at it. The complex sat on top of a hill with a gorgeous view of the city. The design was modern and of a beautiful traditional architecture. Each building had a nice foyer with a huge brass chandelier. It was nice—very nice. Any condo in this complex would certainly be new, nice, and somewhat expensive.

The unit listed with the tax lien was unit 10, so I went to that building. While I might not be able to go inside the unit, at least it would give me the comfort of knowing that I saw unit "10" on the door. But I had one small problem: all of the buildings were secured (I told you it was nice!). Outside of each building was a keypad listing the last names of the tenants to open the front door. Now I had a dilemma: I couldn't get inside the building. Do I follow my rule of always visually inspecting every property, or do I rely on the quality of the building and complex? A stickler for rules, I decided to insist on seeing the unit. Since I knew I couldn't get in without a code, I waited for someone to exit the building. About 10 minutes later, someone came out and I gracefully entered.

The building was not large, so I knew it would just take a minute to find unit 10. I just turned right and walked down the hall. The units were all numbered sequentially. I saw units 1, 2, 3, 4, and 5 and this side ended. Going the other way, I saw that I was headed in the right direction. Unit 6, 7, 8, 9 . . . end of hall. Hmmm, did I go the wrong way? I went back the other way again, and sure enough, that side ended at unit 5. Guess what? There was no unit 10! My guess is that a unit 10 existed in the original architectural plans filed with the county when the complex was built. But it was never built. The county was selling a lien on something that did not even exist! What's worse, the building was secure and most people would not have waited around to get in.

Obviously, a county assessor never visited the property. Nevertheless, it was listed with a value and a tax due just like all the other units. Had I not stuck with my rule of always visually inspecting every property, I would have bought that property and been a very *un*happy camper! Always, always, always visually inspect every property that you intend to buy at a tax deed sale.

ENVIRONMENTAL PROBLEMS

While the vast majority of properties sold at deed sales do not have environmental issues, you will eventually run across a property that does have some issues. In almost all cases, the county will put a special note next to that property indicating that it either has or may have an environmental problem. Figure 11.1 shows such a case from a sale I went to in Los Angeles. If you see something like this, you obviously don't bid on it!

Is it possible to get a property that has an environmental issue but was not flagged by the county? Yes, you could get a property like that if the county did not know of the problem. Here's an easy way to stay clear of these potential problems. One, visually inspect the property. Two, don't buy a gas station property or a property next to a gas station. Three, buy liens only on residential or commercial properties with buildings. Stay away from vacant lands, especially those with industrial zoning.

FIGURE 11.1 *Property Listing Showing Potential Environmental Problem*

```
                                                    MB   PG   PCL
   ITEM        LEGAL  LATEST                      LASTEST  PARCEL
    NO   NSB#  DESC   ASSESSEE    LOCATION    MIN BID.  IMPS EARLIEST PARCEL


   3719   176     E  J   BALDWIN'S   FIFTH   $87,553    Y     8741 011 002
         SUBDIVISION OF  A   PORTION   OF                  81/8741 011 002
         RANCHO LA PUENTE LOT  COM  AT  S
         TERMINUS OF A COURSE IN  W  LINE
         OF VALINDA AVE  PER  MB533-48-49
         HAVING A BEARING OF S 0¢39'50" W
         AND A LENGTH OF 473.38 FT   TH   N
         0¢39'50" E TO A PT N 0¢39'50"   E
         150 FT FROM E PROLONGATION OF   N     THIS PROPERTY MAY BE CONTAMINATED
         LINE OF MAPLEGROVE ST PER CSB119      INVESTIGATE BEFORE YOU PURCHASE
         TH N 86¢02'49" W   150   FT   TH   S
         0¢39'50" W TO SD  N  LINE  TH  E
         THEREON TO A PT  S  47¢18'35"   W
         23.44 FT FROM BEG TH N 47¢18'35"
         E TO BEG   PART   OF   LOT   349
         ASSESSED   TO    SEIRAFI,MOHAMED
         LOCATION COUNTY OF LOS ANGELES
```

INTERNAL REVENUE SERVICE LIENS

In Chapter 7, I discussed the situation with IRS liens. In almost all cases, a tax deed property with an IRS lien will be disclosed by the county. Figure 11.2 shows a list of properties with IRS liens on them. This was disclosed by Los Angeles County in the front of its deed sale catalog. My advice is to just skip these properties!

Because most counties will disclose this information, it is easy enough to avoid these properties. If you end up with a property that does have an IRS lien on it, the IRS has 120 days to act on that lien. Since you are not the debtor (owing the IRS money), the IRS will often exclude the property from its list of assets for the debtor if you ask. In some cases, you may want to discuss the matter with your attorney. Just remember that the IRS must redeem the property within the 120-day window (from the date of the sale) or lose its lien against the property. See Chapter 7 to review.

FIGURE 11.2 *List of Properties with IRS Liens*

2001B IRS LIEN

Item #	Parcel #	Item #	Parcel #	Item #	Parcel #
74	2537 012 006	93	2569 010 003	114	2644 026 004
124	2819 019 005	130	2825 014 057	131	2825 018 045
294	3064 016 040	371	3084 014 018	377	3089 005 003
385	3089 028 029	386	3091 004 009	400	3109 002 075
410	3116 011 019	413	3117 005 036	414	3117 005 037
415	3117 005 038	416	3117 005 039	425	3123 013 036
432	3137 005 029	440	3145 031 040	477	3214 031 013
518	3228 026 014	529	3234 012 003	530	3234 012 004
550	3247 027 001	551	3248 021 025	552	3248 021 045
611	3270 006 007	617	3270 014 011	621	3270 017 047
657	3278 007 001	662	3278 015 031	663	3278 015 032
696	3310 006 005	697	3310 006 041	710	3310 023 009
713	3310 023 020	715	3310 023 024	716	3310 023 025
725	3314 007 064	731	3314 008 068	750	3316 002 001
759	3316 012 008	761	3316 012 048	774	3316 014 041
780	3316 018 051	782	3316 020 044	825	3318 014 062
838	3322 009 022	854	3322 016 003	857	3322 021 038
883	3326 002 117	884	3326 002 127	888	3326 004 053
894	3326 005 084	910	3326 011 063	921	3326 015 068
932	3326 024 001	936	3326 026 014	975	3334 011 033
993	3336 005 052	1004	3336 011 019	1008	3338 002 022
1011	3338 006 021	1057	3346 008 065	1073	3346 022 003
1105	3350 019 014	1109	3350 020 072	1142	3362 006 004
1156	3363 004 029	1158	3363 010 018	1184	3366 012 017
1220	3370 001 028	1224	3370 009 022	1233	3372 004 025
1255	3374 020 021	1265	3376 006 012	1266	3376 010 020
1354	4031 027 014	1363	4061 013 007	1386	4337 020 007
1389	4350 003 007	1395	4371 001 002	1396	4371 003 004
1398	4371 020 017	1404	4371 032 011	1405	4371 036 009
1414	4379 013 006	1427	4380 017 019	1498	4440 003 003
1502	4440 017 001	1521	4442 008 011	1530	4442 014 011
1558	4442 030 014	1574	4444 011 013	1603	4451 011 007
1634	4461 017 046	1636	4461 018 023	1639	4461 018 038
1642	4461 023 003	1647	4461 027 017	1677	4465 005 009
1678	4465 005 024	1775	4490 006 019	1778	4493 001 009
1797	5024 013 011	1810	5037 002 006	1819	5049 013 044
1827	5058 023 046	1851	5137 018 011	1853	5142 016 012
1870	5155 012 178	1892	5207 024 014	1900	5208 013 018
1932	5209 014 010	1943	5209 021 021	1956	5213 023 006
1979	5216 013 017	1985	5217 003 008	1989	5217 011 007
1990	5217 011 008	1993	5217 015 016	1994	5217 015 017
1995	5217 015 018	2010	5225 020 012	2035	5228 019 008
2039	5228 023 011	2052	5243 005 009	2063	5243 007 005
2055	5244 025 005	2096	5302 027 001	2102	5304 004 017
2123	5305 026 035	2125	5305 029 006	2152	5355 009 028
2158	5364 018 019	2166	5381 018 019	2182	5405 007 026
2185	5405 004 016	2191	5415 008 018	2192	5415 008 026

In short, the risks associated with deed investing are all avoidable. Just remember to always see the property before bidding. If you have an interest in a vacant lot, visit the county to see if a property is buildable. County rules vary here, so check with the county first. I once found a lot that was 55 feet wide, but the county's minimum for building was 60 feet. The time to ask the county about this is *before* you bid at the auction, not after you own the property!

LARRY'S REMINDERS

- Counties are ruthless in selling worthless properties at tax deed sales. Always, always, *visually* inspect every property that you intend to buy at a tax deed sale.
- In almost all cases, counties will disclose if a property has, or may have, environmental problems or issues. *Do not bid on these properties.*
- Most counties will also disclose if a property is encumbered by an IRS lien. While your property tax lien will not be extinguished by an IRS lien, I would also avoid these properties.

12

THE BIDDING BATTLE— NOT FOR THE TIMID

Bidding at tax lien and deed auctions is fun, if not exhilarating. Because it is an auction where you bid against others, your competitive juices may start flowing. That can be both good and bad. Active competition tends to focus your attention and heighten your reflexes. However, competition often encourages us to win, which might lead us to bid above our planned figure in the heat of battle. Most of the people at the auction will be seasoned investors. A few will be rookies, and a few more will be at their first sale. Most important, the sale will move very, very fast. If you have seen auctions where professional auctioneers are used, you'll get the point. In fact, some counties employ professional auctioneers to run the sale. So, let's look at a few points for preparing for the auction.

DO YOUR HOMEWORK

In my estimation, 90 percent of mistakes made at deed auctions are due to the bidder's lack of due diligence, or homework.

Some bidders never look at the property. This is the biggest mistake of all, as I discussed previously. Here's my checklist of things to do before the sale.

1. Check the file for the property at the county offices. For a tax deed sale, counties will usually have a big file on each property. This file will normally include information about the taxes due, the owner, and other liens. Sometimes, the file will also have an appraisal from the assessor's office, and sometimes a survey. Normally, the file also will reveal if the property is a vacant lot or an improved lot (i.e., with a building on it). The file may also reveal if the property is a homestead property. If so, there's a great chance that the property tax lien will be paid before the deed sale. In some cases, you also can get detailed information, such as the number of bedrooms and baths, the square feet, year built, and so on. Check to see if the assessor's information is available online as well. I like properties where the monies due (normally the starting point for bidding) are no more than 20 percent of the assessed value. Recall that property taxes are about 1 to 2 percent of the fair market value, and that you will be paying two or more years of back taxes (in most jurisdictions). The county will also add administrative fees and costs.

2. Contact the assessor's office for "comps." Comparables, or sales of comparable properties in the area, will assist you in knowing what you can resell the property for. If the assessor's information is online, the comps can be seen oftentimes there as well.

3. If a vacant lot, locate the physical address. In many instances, a vacant lot will not have a street address. Instead, the county will have a legal address and a parcel identification number. Ask the county official to help you at this point. Normally, you'll go to a plat map to locate the property. You can usually locate the vacant property by the physical street address of the adjacent properties.

4. Now check out the property. Once you have done your homework on the property, you can proceed to view the property. This means you have determined that the property either has a structure on it or is a vacant lot of buildable size. You've looked at the value vis-à-vis the assessed or appraised value. You've made a determination that the property is a good one and that you might be able to get it for a reasonable price. What is reasonable will vary for each person. Those really wanting to "steal" it will look for 10 cents on the dollar. Those who may be in the business of rehabbing and flipping properties may be willing to go up to 50 cents on the dollar or more.

Now a word about when to check out a property. You really should look at all properties a day or two before the sale. Leave a business day before the sale in case you have any questions about the property. Why wait until a few days before the sale? Because at least one half of the properties will redeem just before the sale. If you see six properties you really like, you'll probably only have three to bid on at the sale. So, if you don't want to spend time driving around town looking for the three properties that were not even at the sale, wait until a day or so before the sale.

For example, if the sale is on a Wednesday, go by the county office to look at the files on Monday, and look at the properties Tuesday morning. If the sale is on a Monday, go by the county on Friday and look at the properties late Friday or Saturday. Many counties will show their updated listings on the Internet, so that you can first check there to see if a property has redeemed and been taken off the sale list.

SET YOUR MAXIMUM AHEAD OF TIME

At every deed sale I've been to, there are always some properties that sell for more than they should have. This occurs for two reasons. First, the bidder did not set a maximum price before the sale that he or she would bid. Second, the bidding moves fast and people want to *win*! The bidding is normally competitive and people get excited. You'll be surprised what people will do in the heat of the bidding battle. Here is one more reason why people bid more than they should. Let's say you come to an auction intent on bidding on four properties. One redeems just before the sale, so now you're down to three. The first one comes up and you're outbid. The second one comes up and again you're outbid. As the third and last one comes up, you're likely saying to yourself, "By golly, I'm not going to be outbid on this one! I'm going to go home with something!" Don't do it! There will be other properties and other auctions. Stay the course with your guidelines.

BE ASSERTIVE!

Like lien auctions, deed auctions move fast and only people who are ready with their number and final bid will stay in the game. When it's time for you to jump in, you have to yell your bid as if someone has just stolen your wallet or purse! This goes for lien bidding, too. I've seen too many properties missed because the bidder was too timid in his or her bid. I've trained several people how to do this, and, without exception, the first mistake they all make is to either hesitate with their bid or to say it as if they were talking to the person next to them. Yell it!

WHAT SOME SEASONED INVESTORS DO

Here's the scenario. Say you have a nice property worth $75,000. Suppose the bidding starts at $8,000. You have five bidders actively going at it: "$9,000 . . . $10,000 . . . $10,500 . . . $11,000 . . . $11,500 . . . $12,000. . . ." At this point, we're down to three bidders: "$13,000 . . . $13,400 . . . $13,800. . . ." Now there are only two bidders: "$14,000 . . . $14,300 . . . $14,500 . . . $14,700. . . ." Silence. The auctioneer then says, "$14,700 going once, $14,700 going twice. . . ." Then, from the back of the room: "$20,000." What? Where did that come from? A new bidder! Where's this guy been? He hasn't said a word the whole time and just now comes in, some

$5,300 over the last bid! The guy who has been bidding all along and thought he was going to get it at $14,700 just winces. This new guy, this "mole" in the back of the room, just got it at $20,000, while everyone else in the room stares in shock.

What just happened? The late-entry bid is common bidding practice for some seasoned investors who think that with more bidders, the more a frenzy builds and the higher the price will eventually go. So they sit back and let the other investors weed themselves out. At the final moment, when bidding has stopped, they jump in at a huge increase in bid. So they've done two things. First, they didn't add to the bidding frenzy. Second, they gauged their bid to *shock* the last bidder, who was about to win. Before the last bidder can readjust his or her thinking to this new bid of $20,000 and consider whether to stay in the game, the bidding is over. It's a shrewd strategy, and I see it at almost every deed auction I attend. Be aware of this strategy, either to recognize it, or to use it to your advantage!

LARRY'S REMINDERS

- Do your homework before the sale:
  —Check the file for the property at the county offices.
  —Contact the county assessor's office for comps.
  —If a vacant lot, locate the physical address.
  —Personally inspect the property.
- Set your maximum bid ahead of time.
- Be assertive—yell out your bid as if someone has robbed you.
- Be aware of the late bidding "shock" investors and their strategy.

13

FREE AND CLEAR, BUT CAN I SELL IT?

Whenever you acquire a property through either a tax lien or tax deed scenario, you have both good news and bad news. The good news is that you typically own it free and clear. The better news is that you probably bought it for somewhere between pennies on the dollar and 50 cents on the dollar. The bad news is that your title is not the same as when you buy a house through a normal sale with an individual seller. Actually, it's not bad news; it just means you may need to do a little bit of work to "perfect the title."

PERFECTING THE TITLE

When you acquire a property from a taxing entity, you are not getting the same title as you would if you just bought a property from an individual seller. In the individual-to-individual scenario, the buyer will demand a certain type of deed, namely a "warranty" deed. What that means is that the seller is giving you a warranty (or guarantee, if you will) that the title is good, marketable, and insurable. Essentially, this means that the title is "clean," or free from any encumbrances (or the title company may "except" an encumbrance from coverage in its title insurance policy).

In a property acquired from the county, however, you will not receive a warranty deed. The county is not giving you *any* warranties. That's not its job. The county tax collector or treasurer is not a title insurance company. The county official's job is to collect the taxes due on that property. Period. You typically will get a *sheriff's deed, tax deed, constable's deed,* or similar deed of conveyance. Figure 13.1 shows a copy of the sheriff's deed I received on the house I bought at the Kansas deed sale.

If you plan to resell the property for full fair market value (called a "retail" sale in real estate lingo), however, most title companies will not accept this type of deed. You likely will need to have an attorney file what is called a "quiet title action." This is a fairly simple "pleading" that the attorney will file with the local court. If anyone claims to have rights in the property, he or she will have to respond to this pleading or forever lose any potential rights. Absent a scenario where you acquired a deed before a redemption period had run, it is highly unlikely anyone will claim rights at this point. Depending on your area of the country, you may pay an attorney $1,000 to $3,000 to do this. Once this is completed, you will be able to sell the property with a warranty deed and can ask for full fair market value. Since you acquired the property far below fair market value, spending another thousand dollars or so to perfect the title should not bother you. You simply need to factor in this amount as a cost of doing business, the same way you would consider brokers' commissions.

However, if you buy a property for 10 to 50 cents on the dollar, you may want to consider selling the property "wholesale" to a "retail" seller. A retail seller is someone who wants to rehab the property and sell it for fair market value. These retail sellers generally buy properties for 50 to 75 cents on the dollar from wholesalers.

FIGURE 13.1 *Example of Sheriff's Deed*

SHERIFF'S DEED

KNOW ALL MEN BY THESE PRESENTS, THAT a certain action to foreclose tax liens on certain real property in the County of Leavenworth, State of Kansas, has heretofore been filed in the District Court of Leavenworth County, Kansas, and is titled: The Board of County Commissioners of Leavenworth County, Kansas v. JL Clark Plumbing & Heating, Inc, et al, Case No. 0107 CV 224; and Judgement was thereafter rendered by said court in the above entitled action on 19 October, 2001.

In compliance with, and pursuant to this Judgment, the Clerk of the District Court of Leavenworth County, Kansas, issued an order to Sheriff Herbert F. Nye, Sheriff of Leavenworth County, Kansas, to advertise and sell tracts of land, lots, or pieces of real estate described below, all according to law.

The Leavenworth County Sheriff gave notice of this sale by advertisement and publication notice of sale in The Tonganoxie Mirror newspaper printed in Leavenworth County, Kansas, and which had been continuously and uninterruptedly published in Leavenworth County, Kansas, not less than fifty (50) weeks for a period of five years prior to the first publication notice, all according to the law. The Leavenworth County Sheriff, Herbert F. Nye, thereafter sold to Larry Boyd Loftis for the highest and best bid obtainable on 11 December, 2001, the following described real property; for the amount shown by each particular tract, lot, or piece of real estate.

DESCRIPTION: The South Half of Lot 26, and all of Lots 27 and 28 in Block numbered 33, Macaulay's First Addition to the City of Leavenworth according to the recorded plat thereof.

Entered in the transfer record in my office this ___19___ day of _Dec_ 20_01_

Linda Scheer by J. Klaoneski
County Clerk

Price: $4,100.00

THEREAFTER, on the 17th day of December, 2001, the order of sale and the proceedings of sale were returned to the Leavenworth County District Court and after examination of the proceedings, and finding that the sale was made in all respects in conformity with the law applicable, the District Court of Leavenworth County confirmed the sale, and the proceedings made thereto, on the 18th day of December, 2001.

THEREAFTER, and according to law, the Sheriff of Leavenworth County was ordered to execute this good and sufficient deed to the purchaser(s) Larry Boyd Loftis.

I, Herbert F. Nye, Sheriff of Leavenworth County, Kansas, therefore do hereby give, grant, sell and convey to Larry Boyd Loftis, their heirs and assigns, forever, all the above-described real estate located in Leavenworth County, Kansas, together with all and singular tenements, hereditaments and appurtenances thereto or in any way appertaining, subject to zoning regulations, easements, restrictions, and mineral interests of record.

TO HAVE AND TO HOLD THE SAME UNTO THE SAID Larry Boyd Loftis, their heirs and assigns forever.

IN WITNESS WHEREOF, I, Herbert F. Nye, Sheriff of Leavenworth County, State of Kansas, have hereunto set my hand this _18th_ day of December, 2001.

Herbert F. Nye
Sheriff of Leavenworth County, Kansas

STATE OF KANSAS   )
)   SS:
COUNTY OF LEAVENWORTH   )

    This instrument was acknowledged before me the _18th_ day of December, 2001 by Herbert F. Nye as Sheriff of Leavenworth County, Kansas.

K. Janette Nessmith - Eyerly
Notary Public - State of Kansas
My Appt. Expires 01-24-2004

Notary Public

My Appointment Expires:
01-24-2004

Have you ever seen the signs that say, "We Buy Ugly Houses"? These are wholesalers. They will advertise to find people in a real jam who need to sell a house quickly. They'll buy these ugly (because they need work) houses quickly with cash. Then they'll put an ad in the paper that says something like "Handyman Special." This ad will draw out the retailers who want to buy it for 75 to 80 cents on the dollar, fix it up, and resell it for full fair market value.

If you choose this wholesale method, you can sell the property by way of a *quit claim deed*, which gives no warranties. Since you are selling it at a significant discount, buyers know they have plenty of profit margin to work with. Your buyer can later perfect the title if he or she so chooses. In most cases, they'll just invest the $1,000 to $3,000 to file the quiet title action and get a clean deed. You can find rehabbers (or retailers) by advertising a handyman special in the paper, or by attending your local real estate investors' club.

YOU HAVE THE PROPERTY, NOW WHAT?

Once you acquire a property, here are your options: (1) rent the property; (2) sell the property with a broker; (3) sell the property "for sale by owner"; or (4) simply hold it for investment purposes. If you decide to use a broker to resell the property and do not know of anyone in the area, you can probably get a referral from your local title company. Another way is to just use one of the national brokerage firms like Watson, Century 21, or RE/MAX. I have sold a couple of properties using RE/MAX. I like RE/MAX, because it is national but each office is independently owned. The RE/MAX brokers I have used to sell properties have been outstanding.

If you decide to sell the property "by owner," you will eliminate any broker commissions. This may be less practical where the property is not vacant land, however. For example, if you live out-of-state, how will you show the property? If the property is local or is vacant land, the sale by owner also has an additional benefit.

Since you own the property outright, you can sell it with owner financing. For example, you could get, say, 10 percent down (or the amount you paid for the property), and finance the balance at, say, 8 percent for 5, 10, or even 30 years. If you don't want to wait this long, you also can put in a balloon where the balance will be due in three, four, or five years. One thing is certain: If you finance the property, you will sell it faster and can ask a higher price. I used this approach to sell a large home in Orlando. I sold it quickly and got my exact asking price. I've also used a lease option to entice renters/owners (basically renting with an option to buy at some point in the future).

SELLING YOUR REAL ESTATE NOTE

If you choose the seller financing option and take back a mortgage and promissory note from the buyer, you now have another option. You can sell that note for cash. In some cases, you can even do a "simultaneous close," where the sale of the property and the sale of the note occur at the same time. In actuality, the note is sold a few minutes after the property, but the seller leaves with a check in hand for the note.

WHAT NOT TO DO

Let me add one last bit of advice. If you do get a property, whatever you do, don't sit on it. That is, do not just let it sit there without taking some action, whether selling it, rehabbing it, or renting it. If you do sit on a property, three things will happen (I learned this the hard way). First, any improved property that sits without occupants (and air-conditioning) will deteriorate. Rodents may find their way in. If you're in the South, roaches certainly will. Second, weeds will grow. In addition to making the house look unsightly, it will become a health hazard and the county will mow it for you and charge an outlandish fee—like $200 each time. Third, property taxes (and insurance, if you have it) will accrue each month, just adding up month after month. If you let a property sit for months, you'll quickly be eating into your original profit margin. In short, decide what you want to do with the property and get on it!

LARRY'S REMINDERS

- If you acquire a property at a tax deed sale, you will not acquire it with warranties.
- If you want to resell the property for full fair market value, you will need to "perfect" the title.
- Perfecting the title will require hiring an attorney to "quiet the title."
- If you want to sell the property quickly, consider selling it wholesale to a "retailer" through a quit claim deed.
- Never sit on a property after acquiring it. Your property will deteriorate and each day will mean costs in insurance and mowing.

LIST OF STATES

ALABAMA

Sale Type:	Lien
Interest Rate:	12% per annum
Bid Method:	Premium bid (premium also receives 12%)
Redemption Period:	3 years
Sale Date(s):	May
Statute Section(s):	Code of Alabama Sections 40-10-15, 20, 120, 121, 187
Over-the-Counter?	Yes (See "Comments")

Comments:

Alabama has over-the-counter sales (called "sold to state" properties) for both tax lien certificates and tax deeds. These sales are handled on the state level. Tax certificates not purchased at the county level are delivered to the Alabama Commissioner of Revenue. You may contact the state commissioner at:

Alabama Department of Revenue
Property Tax Division
P.O. Box 327210
Montgomery, AL 36132-7210

ALASKA

Sale Type:	Deed
Interest Rate:	N/A
Bid Method:	Set by municipality
Redemption Period:	1 year minimum (set by municipality)
Sale Date(s):	Varies by municipality
Statute Section(s):	Alaska Statutes, Chapter 48
Over-the-Counter?	No

Comments:

Alaska is a bit different than most deed states in two respects. First, the only "bidders" at a tax sale are the municipalities. Properties are generally transferred to the municipalities for the lien amount. Thereafter, a minimum redemption period of one year must transpire. Properties then may be sold by the municipalities under procedures set by local ordinance. Second, the sale by the municipality likely will set the sale price at the fair market value.

Thus, Alaska is *not* one of the better deed states.

ARIZONA

Sale Type:	Lien
Interest Rate:	16% per annum
Bid Method:	Bid down the interest
Redemption Period:	3 years (if judicial foreclosure)
	5 years (if nonjudicial foreclosure)
Sale Date(s):	February
	Coconino (Flagstaff)—3rd Thursday
	Maricopa (Phoenix)—online sale (2007 sale was February 1)
Statute Section(s):	Arizona Revised Statutes Sections 42-312, 390, 393, 410, 451, 462
Over-the-Counter?	Yes
Comments:	

In Arizona, *the tax lien does NOT take priority over a* state *lien.* As such, you could foreclose on your tax lien and get the property, only to find out that there was a large lien held by the State of Arizona, which would run with the land. Check with the county involved to be sure there is no state lien (or a very small one) on your property before purchasing the lien.

ARKANSAS

Sale Type:	Deed
Interest Rate:	N/A
Bid Method:	Premium bid
Redemption Period:	30 days (from auction date)
Sale Date(s):	May 1 (Little Rock)
Statute Section(s):	Arkansas Code, Chapter 38

Over-the-Counter?   No
Comments:

In Arkansas, the minimum bid for a tax deed property is not only the lien amount (i.e., delinquent property taxes, penalties, interest, and costs), but also the county assessor's assessed value. Under Arkansas law, the assessed value of a property is 20% of the assessor's "true market value." Since property taxes typically run 1% to 2% of the property's value, the minimum that you could purchase a property for would likely be 25%. Check also to see the number of years of delinquent property taxes.

CALIFORNIA

Sale Type:	Deed
Interest Rate:	N/A
Bid Method:	Premium bid
Redemption Period:	N/A
Sale Date(s):	Varies by county
	Fresno—1st Monday in March
	Kern (Bakersfield)—March/July/November (online)
	Los Angeles—February/August
	San Diego—February
	San Francisco—April
Statute Section(s):	California Revenue and Taxation Code
	Chapter 7, Sections 3691, 3698, 3712
Over-the-Counter?	No

Comments:

1. A property acquired at a tax deed sale in California would be acquired *free of all liens and encumbrances,* except for any special assessments, easements (which always run with any property upon conveyance), and possibly an IRS lien. In the vast majority of cases, none of these items is present, so the property may be acquired for as little as pennies on the dollar (bidding permit).

2. I purchased one property a few years ago in Los Angeles and bid on several others. There was an enormous amount of properties sold (over 3,900 properties in the sale book, although probably half of those redeemed and half of those remaining were bad properties). My guess is that about 1,000 good properties were sold. There appeared to be 300 to 400 bidders at

the sale. For improved properties (i.e., those with a house or other building on them), the bidding was fairly active. The property I purchased (my assistant purchased one also) was a vacant lot and was bought at the opening bid. As it turned out, the assessor's appraised value was far above what my California broker says it can be sold for (but far in excess of what I paid, $900). Beware of erroneous assessor values!

3. *Carefully inspect your properties beforehand!* I also tried to look at several lots that were impossible to find because of their remote mountain location, or were probably unsuitable for building due to mountain conditions. The county is irresponsible for selling these, but they do anyway. *Always, always, check out the property closely before you bid on it.*

COLORADO

Sale Type:	**Lien**
Interest Rate:	9 points above the federal discount rate set in September, rounded to the nearest full percent. In 2006, this rate was 15 percent (2007 was not determined as of this writing). See "Comments" on the effect of premium bidding.
Bid Method:	Premium bid (See "Comments")
Redemption Period:	3 years
Sale Date(s):	1st Thursday in November
	Jefferson County (Golden)—online sale (October)
Statute Section(s):	Colorado Revised Statutes, Sections 39-12-103, 39-11-120, 122
Over-the-Counter?	Allowed (but not mandatory) by statute; check with each particular county. Denver is "no."

Comments:

NOTE: Under Colorado's premium bidding system, *the investor does NOT receive back any premium bid over the lien amount or any interest thereon.* For example, suppose the lien amount was $1,000. If an investor bid $1,500 for that lien, he would receive his interest rate only on the $1,000. He would *LOSE* the $500 premium and receive no interest on that amount. Since this system certainly reduces the attractiveness to investors, some counties utilize the *rotational* bidding system.

CONNECTICUT

Sale Type:	Deed (a hybrid state; see "Comments")
Interest Rate:	18% per annum
Bid Method:	Premium bid (premium also receives 18%)
Redemption Period:	1 year
Sale Date(s):	June
Statute Section(s):	General Statutes of Connecticut Section 12-157
Over-the-Counter?	No

Comments:

Technically, Connecticut is a deed state with a one year right of redemption. However, it operates much more like a lien state. Within two weeks after the tax sale, the county collector will execute a deed to the purchaser or municipality; however, this deed will not be recorded for one year (the redemption period). If the owner redeems, he or she pays the total amount paid by the purchaser, plus 18% per annum. If the owner does not redeem, the deed is recorded and the purchaser gets the property.

In some areas (e.g., New Haven), the city collects the taxes and sells the liens. However, New Haven only sells them to qualified buyers in very large bulk sales.

DELAWARE

Sale Type:	Deed (a hybrid state; see "Comments")
Interest Rate:	15% penalty (See "Comments")
Bid Method:	Premium bid
Redemption Period:	60 days
Sale Date(s):	Varies by county (only 3)
	Kent County—Jan., Apr., July, Oct.
	Sussex County—varies (3 or 4 per year)
	New Castle—varies
Statute Section(s):	9 Del. Code Sections 8721, 8728, 8749, 8750, 8758
Over-the-Counter?	No

Comments:

1. Delaware is a deed state but operates like a lien state (thus, it's a hybrid state).

2. Delaware is a very interesting state. I spoke with the county attorney who has handled the sale for Sussex County for several years. The state's statutes give the counties more than one way to execute their tax sales. For example, Section 8776 of Title 9 (9 Del. C. § 8776) provides one way to execute their sale—20% interest with a one-year redemption. However, Sections 8728 and 8758 allow for another system—the one actually used by the counties. Under this system, the owner has only *60 days* to redeem, it is a *15% penalty,* and it is a priority lien (i.e., ahead of all other liens and extinguishes them). Once the sale is completed, the county attorney will petition the Superior Court for an order approving the sales. This will be a routine matter unless a mistake or some extraordinary event occurred. Once the sale is approved by the court, the 60-day period begins.

3. Recall how the penalty system works. The owner must pay that penalty, regardless of when the lien is redeemed. Accordingly, the faster the owner pays, the greater your rate of return. Now let's examine the rate of return under the system used in Delaware—15% penalty and 60-day redemption period. Let's assume that it took the county attorney a month to get the court approval. What's your rate of return?

Month	Activity	Return if Redemption after End of Month
1	Court approval	180%
2	1st 30 days	90%
3	2nd 30 days	60%

You determine your rate of return by multiplying the percentage received each month by the number of months per year (12). Thus, in month one, you received 15% times 12 = 180. If redemption occurred after two months, you still get the same amount (i.e., 15%), but it now took two months to receive. Thus, you received 7.5% each month times 12 = 90.

DISTRICT OF COLUMBIA

Sale Type: Lien

Interest Rate: 18% per annum

Bid Method:	Premium bid (premium does *not* receive interest)
Redemption Period:	6 months (See "Comments")
Sale Date(s):	July
Statute Section(s):	D.C. Code Section 47-1304
Over-the-Counter?	No

Comments:

1. Redemption: The six-month redemption period is not self-executing. After waiting four months, the investor may order a title search on the property from a qualified title company. After six months, and upon completion of the title search, the investor may file an action with the District of Columbia Superior Court to foreclose the owner's right of redemption.

2. Sale observations: I attended and bought liens at the 2001 sale. I made two observations from the sale. First, most of the properties were bid at premiums, thus reducing the investor's yield below 18%. In D.C., the premium does not receive the 18% interest. For example, an investor buying a $1,000 lien for $2,000 would only receive a 9% rate of return, since the $1,000 premium received no interest at all. On average, most investors were willing to accept a 9% to 10% return. I wanted the 18% returns, so I purchased liens on vacant lots (less interest from bidders). One lot was actually owned by a local college.

The second observation I made was how *unfriendly and unprofessional* the city employees were. While there were probably four to six city employees standing (or sitting) around at all times, none of them could assist with any questions. All of the government workers said questions would have to be answered by the tax sale manager, Connie Hogue. However, Ms. Hogue stayed out of sight for most of the sale and refused to meet with or answer questions from investors. I never even saw her. Given the city's objective to sell liens, I found this very unusual. I have attended lien and deed sales all over the country. Most city and county officials are courteous and helpful. A few are not. The D.C. employees are the worst of those in the latter category.

FLORIDA

Sale Type:	Lien
Interest Rate:	18% per annum, but 5% minimum (See "Comments")
Bid Method:	Bid down the interest

Redemption Period:	2 years
Sale Date(s):	May–June. Most major counties (ie., Orange, Dade, Broward, Hillsborough, West Palm Beach) conduct the sale online.
Statute Section(s):	Florida Statutes Annotated Section 197
Over-the-Counter?	Liens—no; deeds—yes

Comments:

1. Florida Statute Section 197.472(2) provides in pertinent part:

> When a tax certificate is redeemed and the interest amount earned on the certificate is less than 5 percent of the face amount of the certificate, a mandatory charge (i.e., penalty) of 5 percent shall be levied upon the tax certificate. The person redeeming the tax certificate shall pay the interest rate due on the certificate or the 5 percent mandatory charge, whichever is greater.

What this means is that, regardless of the interest rate bid, the investor will get a minimum of a 5% penalty rather than the annualized interest rate. For example, if I purchased the lien at 18%, that is 1.5% per month on an annualized basis. So what if the owner redeems after only one month? I still get an 18% interest rate, but that is not much in actual dollar amount since it is only 1.5%. The Florida legislators realized the disadvantage to investors, so they made sure the investor would get a minimum of 5% return in actual dollars. Thus, if an owner redeems after only one month, the investor realizes a 60% return (5% × 12 months = 60%). I have received not only a 60% return on some of my Florida liens, I also have received an infinite return since one paid off (with a 5% penalty) before I actually went down to the county to pay the invoice for the lien!

If you attend a sale (now online) at a large county like Orange County (Orlando), you'll notice that many of the corporate investors will bid the lien down to ¼%. The reason is because they know that a number of these liens, particularly the larger ones, will pay off in the first or second month. Thus, their overall return is much higher and will balance out those liens that run the full redemption period.

While the Florida counties have an annual lien sale, they also have deed sales. This is because the foreclosure of the tax lien is not "self-executing" (as in Texas, Connecticut, and other states). The lien holder must file for a "tax deed" with the county. The county will then place that property for sale at a tax deed auction, where the actual property will be sold to pay off the lien (with interest, of course). Smaller counties will have deed sales every two months or so, while larger counties will have sales monthly. Orange County typically has two to four deed sales each month. One disadvantage—if the property is a homestead property, the bidding must start at *one-half* of the county's assessed value!

2. Florida's redemption period is two years. However, if your lien does not redeem, *you must file for a tax deed within seven years* (from the date of purchase) or lose your lien (i.e., you've made a nice donation to the county!).

GEORGIA

Sale Type:	Deed (a hybrid state)
Interest Rate:	20% penalty
Bid Method:	Premium bid
Redemption Period:	1 year (not self-executing)
Sale Date(s):	1st Tuesday of each month (large counties)
	Appling (Baxley)—1st Tuesday in October
	Decatur (Bainbridge)—3 or 4 sales per year
	Dougherty (Albany)—1st Tuesday in August
	Fulton (Atlanta)— 1st Tuesday of each month
	Glynn (Brunswick)—1st Tuesday in July
	Ware (Waycross)—1st Tuesday in August
Statute Section(s):	Official Code of Georgia Annotated Sections 48-2-40; 48-3-19, 20; 48-4-42, 45
Over-the-Counter?	No

Comments:

1. Technically, Georgia is a deed state, but it operates much like a lien state. At the tax sale, the property is sold, subject to a one-year right of redemption. Furthermore, foreclosure on the right of redemption is not "self-executing." Rather, after the one-year period expires, the investor must terminate the redemption right by:

   • sending by certified or registered mail a notice to the owner of the property, any occupant of the property, and any other lien holder (or one having any right or interest in the property); and

- publishing in the local newspaper (where the county sheriff advertises) once a week for four consecutive weeks immediately prior to the week of redemption deadline identified in the notice.

2. Since Georgia's 20% rate is a penalty rather than a per annum interest rate, the faster the redemption, the better the rate of return. Here's what your rate of return would look like based on a redemption between months 1 to 12 (rounded to the nearest whole number):

Redemption After Month:	Effective Rate of Return
1	240%
2	120%
3	80%
4	60%
5	48%
6	40%
7	34%
8	30%
9	27%
10	24%
11	22%
12	20%

Recall that the redemption right is not automatically terminated. What happens if the owner does not redeem after one year? If the owner doesn't pay the first year, he or she incurs an additional penalty of 20% for the second year (even though it may be only one day after the one-year period elapses). O.C.G.A. Section 48-4-42 provides in pertinent part:

The amount required to be paid for redemption of property from any sale for taxes . . . shall be the amount paid for the property at the tax sale . . . plus a premium of 20 percent of the amount *for each year or fraction of a year* which has elapsed between the date of sale and the date on which the redemption payment is made. [emphasis added]

Accordingly, if the redemption occurred after 13 months, your rate of return would be 36.9%! However, it gets better than that. Section 48-4-42 goes on to provide:

> If redemption is not made until after the required notice has been given, there shall be added to the redemption price the sheriff's cost in connection with serving the notice, the cost of publication of the notice, if any, and the *further sum of 20 percent* of the amount paid for the property. . . . [emphasis added]

As such, a redemption after the first year and after the notice was given would be required to pay:

- the amount paid for the property at the sale (i.e., your principal investment),
- 20% penalty for year one,
- 20% penalty for year two,
- *20% penalty after notice is given,* or
- 60% in addition to your principal!

Let's assume you have an owner who has not redeemed after the first year and you send out your statutory notices. Assume that the owner redeems after the second month of the second year. Here's what your return would look like:

> 60% ÷ 14 months = 4.2857%/month
> Annualized: 4.2857 × 12 months = 51.43% return!

Overall, then, Georgia is an excellent state. It has the extra work of the statutory notice to terminate the right of redemption but has a sale *monthly* and provides an investor 20% to 120% return!

GUAM (Territory of)

Sale Type: Deed (a hybrid state)
Interest Rate: 12% per annum
Bid Method: Premium bid

Redemption Period: 1 year
Statute Section(s):   11 Guam Law Section 24812
Over-the-Counter?   No

HAWAII

Sale Type: Deed (a hybrid state)
Interest Rate: 12% per annum
Bid Method: Premium bid
Redemption Period: 1 year
Sale Date(s):   Two sales a year, typically June and November or December
Statute Section(s):   Hawaii Revised Statutes Section 246-60
Over-the-Counter?   No
Comments:
1. Not a bad place to mix a little pleasure with business!
2. For Hawaii County, there are two offices (East and West). We contacted the East county office and found out that the West area is the place to get the better properties. According to the county official, if you buy in the East area, "you'll need a jeep to find it!"

IDAHO

Sale Type: Deed
Interest Rate: N/A
Bid Method: Premium bid
Redemption Period: N/A
Sale Date(s):   May
Statute Section(s):   Idaho Statute Sections 31-808; 63-1003 through 63-1011
Over-the-Counter?   No
Comments:
1. Idaho is a "pure" deed state, since you get the actual property after the sale. Since the delinquent taxes are a priority lien, any other liens will be extinguished by a tax deed sale (the exception, as in most other states, would be for lien holders who were not given notice of the sale—a rare occurrence).

2. The *minimum bid* is determined by the county commissioners. The county treasurer will submit a minimum bid recommendation to the commissioners; this minimum bid will include the delinquent taxes (with penalty and interest), pending issue fees, certifications and special assessments, costs of publication of the notice of the sale, and recording fees. In Ada County (Boise), the bid recommendation will also include a current market value for the property as determined by the Ada County assessor.

ILLINOIS

Sale Type:	Lien
Interest Rate:	18% penalty (See "Comments")
Bid Method:	Bid down the interest (penalty)
Redemption Period:	2 to 3 years (See "Comments")
Sale Date(s):	Varies by county
	Cook (Chicago)—Spring
	Champaign (Urbana)—October
	Adams (Quincy)—last Mon. in October
	DuPage (Wheaton)—1st week in December
	Peoria (Peoria)—October
Statute Section(s):	35 Illinois Compiled Statutes 205/238, 200/21-350, 355, 385
Over-the-Counter?	No

Comments:

1. *Redemption period:* Illinois law provides that property sold at a tax sale may be redeemed within two years of the date of the sale. However, if the property sold was improved (i.e., had a house or other structure on it) with one to six units, it may be redeemed within two and one-half years from the date of sale. However, the *purchaser* of property sold at a tax sale may extend the redemption date to three years by filing with the county clerk of court (where the property is located) a written notice describing the property, stating the date of the sale, and specifying the extended redemption time.

2. Notice how the Illinois statute sets forth the payment due, depending upon the redemption time. Statute 35 ILCS 200/21-355 provides in pertinent part:

> Any person desiring to redeem shall deposit with the county clerk . . . an amount equal to the following:

(a) the certificate amount . . .
(b) the accrued penalty, computed through the date of redemption as a percentage of the certificate amount, as follows:

(1) if the redemption occurs on or before the expiration of 6 months from the date of sale, the certificate amount times the penalty bid at sale;

(2) if the redemption occurs after 6 months from the date of sale, and on or before the expiration of 12 months from the date of sale, the certificate amount times 2 times the penalty bid at sale;

(3) if the redemption occurs after 12 months from the date of sale, and on or before the expiration of 18 months from the date of sale, the certificate amount times 3 times the penalty bid at sale;

(4) if the redemption occurs after 18 months from the date of sale, and on or before the expiration of 24 months from the date of sale, the certificate amount times 4 times the penalty bid at sale;

(5) if the redemption occurs after 24 months from the date of sale, and on or before the expiration of 30 months from the date of sale, the certificate amount times 5 times the penalty bid at sale;

(6) if the redemption occurs after 30 months from the date of sale, and on or before the expiration of 36 months from the date of sale, the certificate amount times 6 times the penalty bid at sale.

Now let's examine the potential rates of return, given different redemption times. Assuming that the penalty rate was not bid down (i.e., that you received it at the maximum 18%), here's what you would have (rounded to the nearest whole number):

Year 1

Redemption after Month:	Rate of Return
1	216%
2	108%
3	72%
4	54%
5	43%
6	36%
7	62%
8	54%
9	48%
10	43%
11	39%
12	36%

Year 2

Redemption after Month:	Rate of Return
13	50%
14	46%
15	43%
16	40%
17	38%
18	36%
19	45%
20	43%
21	41%
22	39%
23	38%
24	36%

Year 3

Redemption after Month:	Rate of Return
25	43%
26	42%
27	40%
28	39%
29	37%
30	36%
31	42%
32	40%
33	39%
34	38%
35	37%
36	36%

3. The above numbers are startling. You will not be the first investor to see those returns and say, "Wow, I'm going there!" In addition, since "deep-pocket" investors will want to sink as much money as they can into those kind of returns, expect most areas to bid down that penalty number lower than 18%. The deep-pocket investors *need* to get a lot of liens, because they have a lot of money to place. As such, they're willing to bid the interest rate down to 10%, 9%, 8%, 7%, or even much lower (also knowing that some will redeem in a month or so and they'll get a much better rate of return). What I've found at numerous auctions is that if you are patient (i.e., you may have to sit there for the better part of a day), alert, and willing to get a lien on a vacant lot, you can generally spend what you want and get a decent rate (say, 15% to 17%).

4. In addition to the Annual Tax Sale, Illinois also has a "Scavenger Sale" (conducted in odd-numbered years) for properties that have tax delinquencies for two or more years and were not purchased at the Annual Tax Sale. See the Illinois section of the Appendix for more information.

INDIANA

Sale Type:	Lien
Interest Rate:	10% to 15% penalty (See "Comments")
Bid Method:	Premium bid
Redemption Period:	1 year (See "Comments")
Sale Date(s):	Varies by county (must be Aug., Sept., or Oct.)
	Marion (Indianapolis)—September
	Allen (Ft. Wayne)—September
Statute Section(s):	I.C. 6-1.1-24
Over-the-Counter?	No

Comments:

1. *Interest Rate/Penalty:* Indiana charges a penalty rather than an interest rate, and the amount depends on the redemption time. Indiana law provides that the redemption fee will be calculated as follows:

   1. On the minimum bid:
      - 10% of the minimum bid if redeemed not more than 6 months after the date of the sale.
      - 15% of the minimum bid if redeemed more than 6 months but not more than one year after the date of sale.

   2. On the *difference* between the successful bid price and the minimum bid (referred to as Tax Sale Overbid):
      - 10% per annum interest from the date of payment to the date of redemption.

   Let's start with the minimum bid, or the amount owed to the county and where bidding will begin. If you get any liens at the opening bid (as I did at the 2001 sale in Marion County), your rate of return will be excellent. Since it is a penalty format and is graduated depending on your redemption time, your return is better if the lien is paid off faster. The chart on the next page will set forth your return (rounded to the nearest whole number):

Redemption after Month:	Rate of Return
1	120%
2	60%
3	40%
4	30%
5	24%
6	20%
7	26%
8	22%
9	20%
10	18%
11	16%
12	15%

Like other states with outstanding rates of return, expect competitive bidding on most (not all) liens. As a general rule of thumb in any state, the vacant lots and lower-class houses will get the least amount of competitive bidding (most of the time no bidding at all). If you bid over the lien amount (which is a premium amount but which is called an *overbid*), you will only receive 10% per annum on that overbid amount. For example, if you buy a $1,000 lien for $1,500, you will receive the penalty and rate of return (as set forth on the table above) on $1,000, and 10% simple interest on the premium of $500. As you can see, this overbid will reduce your overall rate of return. However, since your penalty rate is outstanding and 10% on an overbid is not too bad either, you'll probably be happy in any case.

3. *NEW LAW:* Property owners *cannot* redeem after one year (the old system allowed them to redeem after one year and pay a higher penalty). In addition, if the lien is not redeemed after one year, the lien buyer must apply for a tax deed within six months from that expiration date or forfeit his or her purchase money.

4. *Unique bidding system:* The premium system used is not unique. However, how premiums are sold is (at least for the larger counties like Marion). The county official will list a group of 25 liens on an overhead screen. If you desire to bid on any of the liens shown in that group, you must yell out the number of the lien

you wish to pursue. The county official will then reannounce that lien number, the address, and the lien amount, and then open the bidding. If no one bids against you, you get it at the minimum bid (i.e., the lien amount). While this sounds like a chaotic system (since several people could be yelling at the same time), it actually ran very efficiently (probably because of the politeness of the midwestern folks in attendance).

5. *General comments:* I attended the 2001 sale in Marion County (Indianapolis) and found it one of the best run, most professional systems in the country. It ran like clockwork. In addiption, the people were very friendly and very helpful. I suppose it's the midwestern ethic, since the people in Iowa are the same (as opposed to the government employees in Philadelphia and D.C., where officials treat you like you're a nuisance!).

One disadvantage, however, to Indiana is that each county has townships, and each township has its own tax assessor. This makes your research more difficult since the township assessors are not accessible online, and you must go to each township to gather information about any particular property.

6. *New Web site:* Marion County now is making the list of auction properties available online at *www.indygov.org/treas/taxsale/index.htm.*

IOWA

Sale Type:	Lien
Interest Rate:	24% per annum
Bid Method:	Random selection, rotational (See "Comments")
Redemption Period:	2 years (See "Comments")
Sale Date(s):	3rd Monday in June (see also Adjourned Tax Sales below)
Statute Section(s):	Code of Iowa, Chapters 446, 447.13, 448
Over-the-Counter?	No

Comments:

1. *Bid method:* Technically, the state is a "bid down the ownership" state. What this means is that if two or more persons want a particular lien, they can bid down how much of the property will be security for the lien. For example, they can bid down the ownership to 80%. This means that if the property owner does not redeem, the lien holder could foreclose on only 80% of the property! To effectively prosecute the foreclosure, a lien holder would have to file a court

action to sell the property and divide the proceeds 80/20! What a mess, right? Fortunately, county treasurers don't like this system either. I have attended sales in three Iowa counties and spoken with county treasurers in four other counties; *none* of these seven counties used the "bid down the ownership" system. All of these counties used either a random selection or a rotational bidding system. Thank heavens!

2. *Redemption period:* The Iowa foreclosure system is not "self-executing." What this means is that the redemption period does not automatically terminate. The lien holder has a right to file (with the county treasurer) a "90-day Notice of Right of Redemption Affidavit" 1 year and 9 months from the date of the sale. If done at that time, this would give the owner exactly 2 years to redeem and not lose the property.

3. *Cancellation of certificate:* The county treasurer may cancel any lien certificate if the holder has not taken any action (i.e., issued his or her 90-day notice) on the certificate after 3 years from the date of issuance of the certificate. If so, you will have made a nice donation to the county—your lien amount! As you may recall, Florida is the same, although it has a 7-year time frame. Any lawyer will tell you that the law punishes those who "sleep on their rights." That is, if you have legal rights on a particular matter, you either pursue those rights or you will eventually lose them.

4. *Adjourned Tax Sales:* These sales (held on the third Monday in August, October, December, January, March, and May) are for unredeemed certificates where no action is taken to obtain the deed.

5. *General comments:* I found the county officials in all seven Iowa counties that I dealt with to be extremely nice, friendly, and helpful.

KANSAS

Sale Type:	Deed
Interest Rate:	N/A
Bid Method:	Premium bid
Redemption Period:	N/A
Sale Date(s):	Varies by county
	Cowley (Winfield)—December
	Douglas (Lawrence)—May
	Johnson (Olathe)—late fall
	Leavenworth (Leavenworth)—October

Sedgwick (Wichita)—July or August
Shawnee (Topeka)—August
Sumner (Wellington)—May
Wyandotte (Kansas City)—August

Statute Section(s):   K.S.A. Section 79-2801
Over-the-Counter?   No
Comments:

Kansas is one of the best deed states in the country. Counties typically start the bidding for the properties at the lien amounts, although some counties allow you to bid *below* the lien amount! For example, Leavenworth County only requires a $50 minimum bid, and Sedgwick County does not have a minimum bid. Keep in mind, as always, the quality of what you are buying. A few years ago I went to the Kansas City sale and picked up a few vacant lots for $75 each, and one small house for $4,100 (which needed a lot of work).

KENTUCKY

Sale Type:	Lien
Interest Rate:	12% per annum
Bid Method:	Premium bid
Redemption Period:	1 year Sale
Date(s):	April to May
Statute Section(s):	K.R.S. Section 134.460
Over-the-Counter?	No

LOUISIANA

Sale Type:	Deed (a hybrid state)
Interest Rate:	12% per annum plus 5% penalty
Bid Method:	Bid down the interest
Redemption Period:	3 years
Sale Date(s):	January to April

Statute Section(s):   L.R.S. Section 47:2181, 2183
Over-the-Counter?   No
Comments:

If redemption occurred in year one, the rate of return for the investor would be 17% (redemption after 1 year) to 72% (redemption after 1 month). The worst-case scenario would be if redemption occurs just before the end of the redemption period. For example, if redemption occurred after 35 months, the rate of return would be 13.7%.

MAINE

Sale Type: Deed
Interest Rate: N/A
Bid Method: Sealed bid (See "Comments")
Redemption Period: N/A (for the deed sale)
Sale Date(s):   Varies by county
Statute Section(s):   Maine Revised Statutes, Title 36
Over-the-Counter?   No
Comments:

1. Property taxes are collected at the city level, rather than at the county level. Accordingly, city ordinances control the sale procedures. If taxes are unpaid, the city will lien that property. Under state law, the owner has 18 months to redeem. If not redeemed, the redemption period automatically terminates, and the city will now own the property.
2. Once the city owns the property, *the city may retain ownership* or sell the property by way of sealed bid. Additionally, even if the city bids the property, the city can reject all bids as inadequate. Maine, then, is one of the worst deed states (from the investor's perspective).

MARYLAND

Sale Type: Lien
Interest Rate: 6% to 24% (varies by county)
Bid Method: Premium bid

Redemption Period: After 6 months (See "Comments")

Sale Date(s): Varies by county

Baltimore City—May or June

Montgomery—June

Garrett—May

Statute Section(s): Annotated Code of the Public Laws of Maryland Section 14817, 818, 820, 831, 833, 844 (See also county code sections for statutes relating to interest rates)

Over-the-Counter? Yes

Comments:

1. As you can see from the above notes, the state gives the counties (and City of Baltimore) great leeway in administrating their own lien sales. The best areas for rates of return are Baltimore City (24%), Prince George's County (20%), Garrett County (20%), and Montgomery County (20%).

2. *Bid method:* Like many other states, Maryland uses a premium bidding method. However, unlike most jurisdictions, Maryland counties do not require the investor to pay the full amount of the bid at the time of the sale. Rather, the investor need only pay for the opening bid (like other states, comprised of back taxes, penalty, and interest) after the sale, not the *full* amount of his or her bid (which would include the opening bid plus the overbid or premium). So when is that overbid (which they call "surplus" or "residue") to be paid by the investor? If the lien is redeemed, the investor *never* pays the surplus! If the lien is *not* redeemed, the investor must pay the surplus before he or she can foreclose on the lien and get a Treasurer's deed.

3. *Redemption period:* The redemption period in Maryland is not self-executing; the investor must actively pursue redemption by filing a complaint at the county level to foreclose the right of redemption. The investor can do this after six months of the date of the sale.

MASSACHUSETTS

Sale Type: Deed (hybrid state)

Interest Rate: 16% per annum

Bid Method: Premium bid

Redemption Period: 6 months (but not self-executing)

Sale Date(s): (See "Comments")

Statute Section(s):   Annotated Law of Massachusetts Sections 45, 62

Over-the-Counter?   No

Comments:

My staff has contacted several Massachusetts counties, including those for Boston and Cambridge, and was told that these areas *did not have* tax sales! Since we've heard that from more than one county, Massachusetts is probably not a great place to look for investing.

MICHIGAN

Sale Type:	Deed
Interest Rate:	N/A
Bid Method:	Premium bid
Redemption Period:	N/A
Sale Date(s):	Varies by county (See "Comments")
	Saginaw (Saginaw)—August
	Genesee (Flint)—March
	Ingham (Lansing)—infrequent, check
	Kent (Grand Rapids)—infrequent, check
	Wayne (Detroit)—end of May
Statute Section(s):	Public Act 123 of 1999; Act 206 of Public Acts 1893 (Sections 140-143)
Over-the-Counter?	No

Comments:

On July 22, 1999, Michigan enacted a new law (Public Act 123), changing the state from a lien state to a deed state. Each county has the option of administering its own sale, or allowing the state to conduct the sale.

MINNESOTA

Sale Type:	Deed
Interest Rate:	N/A
Bid Method:	Premium bid

Redemption Period: N/A

Sale Date(s):   Varies by county

St. Louis (Duluth)—February, June, October

Statute Section(s):   Minnesota Statutes Sections 281, 282

Over-the-Counter?   Yes (including by mail)

Comments:

1. In St. Louis County, most of the tax-forfeited land is forested.
2. *Financing:* Some counties, like St. Louis, will finance your purchase of these properties. St. Louis finances some purchases on a contract for deed basis for up to ten years at 10% interest.

MISSISSIPPI

Sale Type: Lien

Interest Rate: 18% per annum (on the lien only, *not* on the premium)

Bid Method: Premium bid (See "Comments")

Redemption Period: 2 years

Sale Date(s):   Last Monday in August (lien sale)

First Monday in April (deed sale)

Statute Section(s):   Mississippi Code of 1972, as amended

Sections 27-41-55, 59; 27-45-3

Over-the-Counter?   No

Comments:

1. I bought liens in Jackson at the 2001 sale. While there were about 6,900 liens offered, only about 60 bidders were at the sale.
2. *Interest rate:* Notice that *not only is no interest paid on the premium (overbid), but the premium is not repaid either!* As such, any premium bid over the lien amount would reduce your yield. At the 2001 sale in Jackson, most of the liens were sold at premium bids.

MISSOURI

Sale Type: Lien

Interest Rate: 10% per annum (plus 8% for any subsequent taxes paid)

Bid Method:	Premium bid
Redemption Period:	2 years
Sale Date(s):	4th Monday in August (most counties)
	Jackson county has two sales:
	Independence—September
	Kansas City—October
Statute Section(s):	Missouri Revised Statutes § 140
Over-the-Counter?	No

Comments:

Bidder restriction: A bidder *must be a resident of the county* in which the sale is held. In order for a nonresident (i.e., someone from out of state or even out of county) to bid, that person must designate a resident agent for service of process (like corporations must do in each state) and have that county resident bid for him or her at the auction. Needless to say, this requirement, coupled with the low interest rate, makes Missouri one of the least attractive lien states.

MONTANA

Sale Type:	Lien
Interest Rate:	10% per annum plus a 2% penalty
Bid Method:	Random selection or rotational
Redemption Period:	3 years
Sale Date(s):	July
Statute Section(s):	Montana Code Annotated Sections 15-16-102; 15-18-211 through 216
Over-the-Counter?	Yes

Comments:

Since part of the interest rate is a penalty, a lien redeemed in the first year would yield 12% (redemption after one year) to 34% (redemption after one month). After one year, the yield would be between 10% and 12%, depending on the month of redemption.

NEBRASKA

Sale Type:	Lien
Interest Rate:	14% per annum
Bid Method:	Bid down the ownership, rotational
Redemption Period:	3 years
Sale Date(s):	1st Monday in March
Statute Section(s):	Revised Statutes of Nebraska Sections 77-1807, 1824
Over-the-Counter?	Yes

Comments:
1. *Bid method:* Technically, the state uses a "bid down the ownership" system. However, like Iowa, many counties will use a rotational system, since it is far better for all parties concerned.
2. *Over-the-counter:* I purchased a nice lien over-the-counter in Omaha in the summer of 2001 (at the maximum 14%, of course!).

NEVADA

Sale Type:	Deed
Interest Rate:	N/A
Bid Method:	Premium bid
Redemption Period:	N/A
Sale Date(s):	Varies by county Washoe (Reno)—April
Statute Section(s):	Nevada Revised Statutes Sections 361.590-595
Over-the-Counter?	No

Comments:

Nevada is one of the best deed states, since bidding typically starts at the lien amount (i.e., the back taxes, costs, penalties, and interest), and the tax deed sale will extinguish any other liens such as mortgages and judgment liens (special assessments such as a county's mowing lien survive, as in virtually every other state).

NEW HAMPSHIRE

Sale Type:	Deed
Interest Rate:	N/A
Bid Method:	Premium bid
Redemption Period:	N/A
Sale Date(s):	Varies by county
Statute Section(s):	New Hampshire Revised Statutes Annotated Section 80:24
Over-the-Counter?	No

NEW JERSEY

Sale Type:	Lien
Interest Rate:	18% per annum
Bid Method:	Bid down the interest or premium (See "Comments")
Redemption Period:	2 years
Sale Date(s):	Varies by county
	Atlantic City—December
	Camden—January and June
	Burlington—September
	Trenton—March
Statute Section(s):	New Jersey Code Annotated Sections 54:5-32, 54
Over-the-Counter?	No

Comments:

New Jersey is a bit unusual in its approach to bidding. Generally, the bid method will be "bid down the interest." However, if a bidder bids the interest down to less than 1%, he or she may, in lieu of any rate of interest, offer a premium over the amount of taxes, assessments, or other charges. See New Jersey Code Annotated Section 54:5-32.

NEW MEXICO

Sale Type:	Deed
Interest Rate:	N/A
Bid Method:	Premium bid
Redemption Period:	N/A
Sale Date(s):	Varies by county
Statute Section(s):	New Mexico Statutes Annotated, Chapter 7 (Articles 35-38)
Over-the-Counter?	No

Comments:

New Mexico is *not a priority lien state!* Unlike most deed states, an investor who acquires the property at a tax sale takes the property *subject to any encumbrances* (i.e., a mortgage) on the land. Accordingly, an investor at a New Mexico sale must carefully review the title prior to purchasing the property.

NEW YORK

Sale Type:	Deed
Interest Rate:	N/A
Bid Method:	Premium bid
Redemption Period:	N/A
Sale Date(s):	Varies by county
	Albany—July
	Fulton—August
	St. Lawrence—October
Statute Section(s):	Uniform Delinquent Tax Enforcement Act
Over-the-Counter?	No

Comments:

1. New York may, but is not required to, start the bidding at the back taxes, penalty, and costs (i.e., a starting point of a certain percentage of the tax-assessed value). I was at the sale in St. Lawrence County a few years ago and found a number of decent properties (many were huge blocks of acreage). This particular auction was also a popular one; in my estimation, there were about 150 bidders.
2. The City of New York is also allowed to sell liens.

NORTH CAROLINA

Sale Type:	Deed
Interest Rate:	N/A
Bid Method:	Premium bid
Redemption Period:	N/A
Sale Date(s):	Varies by county
Statute Section(s):	North Carolina General Statutes Chapter 44A
Over-the-Counter?	No

Comments:

North Carolina is one of the better deed states, since bidding begins at the lien amount (back taxes, penalties, and costs). However, the state does have two minor disadvantages:

1. *Court confirmation:* Within three days from the date of the sale, the tax commissioner must provide the local county court with the report of all sales. Within 10 days following this filing by the commissioner, anyone claiming an exception or irregularity to the sale may challenge the sale.
2. *Upset bids:* In addition, anyone desiring to increase the bid amount may do so (called an "upset bid") by filing with the court. For you to do so, you must increase the winning bid by 10% of the first $1,000, plus 5% of any excess above $1,000. If an upset bid is filed, the court will negate the first sale and order a second sale, called a "resale."

NORTH DAKOTA

Sale Type:	Lien
Interest Rate:	12% per annum
Bid Method:	Premium bid
Redemption Period:	3 years
Sale Date(s):	2nd Tuesday in December
Statute Section(s):	North Dakota Century Code, Chapters 57-24, 38
Over-the-Counter?	No

OHIO

Sale Type:	Deed and Lien (See "Comments")
Interest Rate:	18% per annum (for lien sales)
Bid Method:	Premium bid (See "Comments")
Redemption Period:	15 days for deed sale (See "Comments")
Sale Date(s):	Varies by county
	Cuyahoga (Cleveland)—May
	Franklin (Columbus)—Every Friday
	Summit (Akron)—October
Statute Section(s):	Ohio Revised Code Sections 2329.17, 20; 5721.23; 315.251
Over-the-Counter?	No

Comments:

1. *Deed and lien sales:* Ohio is historically a deed state, but actually has both types of sales. Counties with populations of over 200,000 are also allowed to sell lien certificates. Check with each county to see which type of sale it uses.
2. *Minimum bid for deed sales:* Pursuant to Ohio Revised Code Section 2329.17, *no tract of land may be sold for less than two-thirds of the appraised value.* As such, no great deals will be found in Ohio. Based on the foregoing, Ohio would be one of the worst of the deed states for bargain-hunting investors.
3. *Redemption period for deed sales:* An owner may redeem his or her property by payment in full of all taxes and costs until the sale is confirmed by court—approximately 15 days. See O.R.C. Section 5721.23.

OKLAHOMA

Sale Type:	Lien
Interest Rate:	8%
Bid Method:	Random selection or rotational
Redemption Period:	2 years
Sale Date(s):	1st Monday in October (normal sale)
	2nd Monday in June (resale)
Statute Section(s):	68 Oklahoma State Statutes Sections 3107; 3135
Over-the-Counter?	Yes

Comments:

1. The fact that Oklahoma has a very low interest rate is actually a benefit for those looking to acquire properties for pennies on the dollar. The reason for this is because far fewer liens will be sold to investors (who will not accept an 8% return). When that occurs, many properties end up in the county's inventory. I was in Oklahoma City a few years ago, and that area had several thousand properties held in inventory (some with redemption periods remaining, others that can be picked up free and clear from the county).

2. In Oklahoma City's "List of Lands Available," there are some 1,100 properties (as I recall) that one can make a bid to purchase. You can order this list from the county for $23.

3. The downside of this surplus in Oklahoma City is that the county does not have the assessed values listed (or other helpful information, for that matter). What you must do is make an offer to the county for each parcel. The county will then accept or reject that offer, perhaps with a counteroffer. However, since the information on these properties have been deleted from the county assessor's office Web site (*www.oklahomacounty.org*), you must now engage a broker to determine the values. In any event, it's still not a bad opportunity.

OREGON

Sale Type:	Deed
Interest Rate:	N/A
Bid Method:	Premium bid
Redemption Period:	N/A
Sale Date(s):	Varies by county
	Multnomah (Portland)—October or November
Statute Section(s):	Oregon Revised Statutes Section 311
Over-the-Counter?	Some counties in the past have allowed

Comments:

As in Ohio, some counties may set the minimum bid as a percentage of the fair market or assessed value, obviously a disadvantage for an investor looking to buy real estate for a fraction on the dollar. In the past, however, many Oregon counties have *financed* purchases by investors! Check with each county for its rules regarding minimum bids and financing.

PENNSYLVANIA

Sale Type:	Deed (a hybrid state)
Interest Rate:	10% per annum where applicable (See "Comments")
Bid Method:	Premium bid (See "Comments")
Redemption Period:	Possibly 1 year (See "Comments")
Sale Date(s):	Monthly
	Allegheny (Pittsburgh)—1st Monday
	Philadelphia (Philadelphia)—3rd Wednesday
Statute Section(s):	Act of Assembly May 16, 1923, P.L. 207; Act of March 15, 1956, No. 388
Over-the-Counter?	Some small counties have allowed

Comments:

I attended the July 18, 2001, sale in Philadelphia. The following summarizes my notes for that city's sale:

1. *Bidding:* The minimum bid was $800.
2. *Right of redemption:* If the property is legally occupied 90 days prior to the sale, the owner has one year within which to redeem the property by paying the back taxes, and pay the investor the purchase price plus 10% interest. If the property is unoccupied or abandoned, there is no right of redemption.
3. *City administration:* All of the properties I intended to bid on were redeemed just before the sale (and there were some *very* nice properties). Philadelphia seems to be somewhat negligent in getting information back to investors in a timely manner. For example, the county employee informed my office over the phone that there would be 75 properties sold at the sale. However, when I received the list of the 75 properties a few days before the sale, some 11 properties had been listed as "STAYED" (*stayed* is the term used to indicate that the owner was given additional time to pay the lien and the property would not be offered at the sale). So, in actuality, only 64 properties would be sold.

I then went to the city's office to do my research. Unfortunately, the city only had three computers for the public to access the information regarding the properties, which were all taken. After waiting about an hour, I was able to jump on one computer and get the information I needed (i.e., assessed value, type of property, size, etc.). I then drove to inspect about 8 properties.

At the sale, the auctioneer read the "updated" list of stayed properties and those being pulled from the sale. Of the 64 remaining properties, another 34 properties were removed from the sale, including all of the 8 on which I had intended to bid. Out of our initial list of 75 properties, now only 30 properties would actually be sold! The 34 properties were not redeemed by the owners, but were simply pulled from the sale by the city. It was very disappointing, since I had just wasted two days. In addition, with the exception of the District of Columbia tax sale employees (who were extremely difficult to deal with), the Philadelphia city employees were the worst I've seen in the country.

PUERTO RICO (Commonwealth of)

Sale Type:	Lien
Interest Rate:	20% penalty
Redemption Period:	1 year
Comments:	

1. There's good news and bad news with Puerto Rico. The good news is that the high penalty makes Puerto Rico one of the best lien jurisdictions in the country. Since it is a 20% penalty, your rate of return would range from 20% (redemption after 12 months) to 120% (redemption after 1 month) or more (redemption earlier than 1 month)! The bad news is you need to speak Spanish. My Spanish is poor, and I didn't get very far trying to talk to someone about his or her sale. So, officially, it's a good lien jurisdiction. Actually getting information on sales, if available, is another story.

RHODE ISLAND

Sale Type:	Deed (a hybrid state)
Interest Rate:	10% penalty plus 1% penalty for each month after month 6
Bid Method:	Premium bid
Redemption Period:	1 year
Sale Date(s):	August
Statute Section(s):	Rhode Island General Laws Sections 44-9-12, 19, 21; 44-9-8.2, 8.3

Over-the-Counter?   No

Comments:

1. Since Rhode Island operates with a penalty, if you were to acquire a lien without a premium, your rate of return would be between 16% (redemption after 12 months) and 120% (redemption after one month)! I have not been to a sale in this state, but my guess is that bidders are bidding premiums.

2. *Madeline Walker Act of 2006:* Contrary to popular rumor, Rhode Island continues to have tax sales. Under the law (sections 44-9-8.2 and 8.3), however, effective January 1, 2007, the Rhode Island Housing and Mortgage and Finance Corporation will take additional steps to protect against tax deed foreclosure on an owner-occupied residential property. For more information, see the new statutes in the Rhode Island section of the Appendix.

SOUTH CAROLINA

Sale Type:	Lien
Interest Rate:	8% or 12% per annum (See "Comments")
Bid Method:	Premium bid
Redemption Period:	1 year
Sale Date(s):	1st Monday in October, November, or December
Statute Section(s):	South Carolina Statutes Section 12-51-90
Over-the-Counter?	Yes

Comments:

Interest rate: If redemption occurs in the first 6 months, the interest rate is 8%; if redemption occurs in the second 6 months, the interest rate is 12%.

SOUTH DAKOTA

Sale Type:	Lien
Interest Rate:	12% per annum
Bid Method:	Premium bid
Redemption Period:	3 years (within municipality); 4 years (outside municipality)
Sale Date(s):	3rd Monday in December
Statute Section(s):	South Dakota Codified Laws Titles 10 and 44; 10-23-28.

Over-the-Counter?   Yes
Comments:

NOTE: As of July 1, 2006, South Dakota counties may no longer sell tax lien certificates. See new state law section 10-23-28.1 in the South Dakota section of the Appendix.

TENNESSEE

Sale Type: Deed (a hybrid state)

Interest Rate: 10% per annum

Bid Method: Premium bid

Redemption Period: 1 year

Sale Date(s):   Varies by county and year

Knoxville—varies (February, fall)

Nashville—June

Statute Section(s):   Tennessee Code Title 67

Over-the-Counter?   No

TEXAS

Sale Type: Deed (a hybrid state)

Interest Rate: 25% penalty (See "Comments")

Bid Method: Premium bid

Redemption Period: 6 months (nonhomestead, nonagricultural)

2 years for homestead, agricultural

Sale Date(s):   1st Tuesday of each month

Statute Section(s):   Texas Tax Code Section 34.21

Over-the-Counter?   Yes (many counties)

Comments:

1. Texas is a hybrid deed state, which means that it is a deed state but operates like a lien state. In Texas, a winning bidder will receive a deed to the property;

however, that deed is encumbered (i.e., subject to a right of redemption by the owner). For agricultural and homestead properties, the redemption period is 2 years. For nonagricultural and nonhomestead properties, the period is only 6 months!

2. Texas is different from most states in that:
   - it has sales every month (as does Georgia), and
   - the sales are administered by law firms (don't worry, you don't pay the lawyers, the county does). As such, you will need to contact the county for the contact information of the law firm assisting the county.

3. *Effect of a penalty:* In Texas, the 25% is a penalty rather than an interest rate. Second, the penalty is not only on the lien amount but also on your premium and any costs associated with the administration of the lien/deed by the law firm and county. As such, you receive 25% on your aggregate total! This makes Texas one of the best states in the country for investors. Now let's look at the impact of a penalty return. The following chart will illustrate your rate of return on a nonagricultural, nonhomestead property, depending on the date of redemption.

Redemption after Month:	Rate of Return
6	50%
5	60%
4	75%
3	100%
2	150%
1	300%

UTAH

Sale Type:	Deed
Interest Rate:	N/A
Bid Method:	Premium bid
Redemption Period:	N/A
Sale Date(s):	May or June
	Salt Lake City—4th Thursday
	Some counties on 3rd Thursday

Statute Section(s):   Utah Code, Title 59
Over-the-Counter?   No
Comments:

Utah is a good deed state, since bidding typically begins at the lien amount (i.e., back taxes, penalties, interest, and costs).

VERMONT

Sale Type: Lien
Interest Rate: 12% per annum
Redemption Period: 1 year
Sale Date(s):   Varies by county
Statute Section(s):   Vermont Statutes, Title 32, Section 5260
Over-the-Counter?   No

VIRGINIA

Sale Type: Deed
Interest Rate: N/A
Bid Method: Premium bid
Redemption Period: N/A
Sale Date(s):   Varies by county
                            Arlington does not have a sale every year.
Statute Section(s):   Code of Virginia, Title 58, Chapter 32
Over-the-Counter: No
Comments:

Overall, Virginia is a good deed state, since bidding begins at the lien amount (i.e., back taxes, penalties, interest, and costs) and the tax lien is a priority lien (i.e., so long as notice was given to other lien holders, any other liens are wiped out by the sale). The sale must be approved by court confirmation, which is routinely given.

WASHINGTON

Sale Type:	Deed
Interest Rate:	N/A
Bid Method:	Premium bid
Redemption Period:	N/A
Sale Date(s):	Varies by county
	King (Seattle)—December
	Spokane—August
Statute Section(s):	Revised Code of Washington, Chapters 35, 60
Over-the-Counter?	No

Comments:

In the Washington section of the Appendix, you'll see that the King County (Seattle) information sheet states in item #3 that "We do not sell 'tax certificates or deeds' of any nature." Surely the county does sell tax deeds since it advertises for them on December 14, 2007. They just call it a "tax foreclosure" sale (otherwise known as a tax deed sale).

WEST VIRGINIA

Sale Type:	Lien
Interest Rate:	12% per annum
Bid Method:	Premium bid (but not on overbid)
Redemption Period:	17 months
Sale Date(s):	Varies by county between October and November
	Kanawha (Charleston)—November
Statute Section(s):	West Virginia Code Section 11A-3-23
Over-the-Counter?	Liens—no; deeds—yes (See "Comments")

Comments:

1. *Bidding:* Notice that you do not receive any premium on any overbid (i.e., premium or surplus) amount.
2. *Over-the-counter:* If you wish to acquire properties, contact the deputy land commissioner at 304-343-4441. The land commissioner may have his or her own sales for properties owned by the county and may allow purchasing over-the-counter.

WISCONSIN

Sale Type:	Deed
Interest Rate:	N/A
Bid Method:	Premium bid (See "Comments")
Redemption Period:	N/A
Sale Date(s):	Varies by county
	Eau Claire—twice per year (spring and summer)
	Dane (Madison)—not held every year
Statute Section(s):	Wisconsin Statutes, Chapter 75
Over-the-Counter?	No

Comments:

Wisconsin appears to be the least desirable of all the deed states, since the county may not accept bids less than the appraised value. Keep in mind, of course, that sometimes the county's appraised value may be significantly less than the true fair market value.

WYOMING

Sale Type:	Lien
Interest Rate:	15% per annum plus 3% penalty
Bid Method:	Random selection
Redemption Period:	4 years
Sale Date(s):	July, August, September (most in September)
	Laramie (Cheyenne)—1st week in August
	Teton (Jackson)—1st week in August
Statute Section(s):	Wyoming Statutes Sections 39-3-108, 39-4-102
Over-the-Counter?	Yes

A

SAMPLE STATE BIDDING, REGISTRATION, AND SALES RULES

Each state and county has different rules governing tax lien properties. The following pages contain sample information available to the general public from various counties across the country.

CALIFORNIA

KERN COUNTY, CALIFORNIA

Web sites for information:
www.kcttc.co.kern.ca.us/taxsales.cfm
www.kcttc.co.kern.ca.us/salefaq.cfm

Who can place a bid?

Only registered bid4assets.com members can bid on Kern County properties. To register to bid, visit: *www.bid4assets.com.*

What is an autobid?

An autobid (or proxy) saves you time and money. An autobid authorizes Bid4Assets to bid $100 above any competing bid, up to, but not exceeding the maximum dollar amount that you are willing to pay. In other words, your bid will automatically increase ONLY as other bidders participate, up to your specified maximum amount. This enables you to continually bid without having to constantly monitor the auction.

Can I change or cancel a bid?

A bid is an irrevocable offer to purchase the asset. Once submitted, there is no way to cancel a bid.

What is the minimum bid price?

The minimum dollar amount Kern County is willing to accept for an item to be sold at the auction.

What happens when the auction ends?

The winning bidder will receive an Asset Alert stating that the auction has closed. The alert will include the asset description and closing bid price. The winning bidder will need to either wire funds or FedEx a cashier's check made payable to Jackie Denney—KCTTC. The address is: 1115 Truxtun Avenue, Bakersfield, CA 93301. It is your responsibility to complete the sale in accordance with the Terms of Sale in the online Asset Listing.

Is it possible to bid offline?

You must contact bid4assets.com's Client Services Department at 1-877-427-7387. You will be registered to bid and will then receive the Offline Bid Form either by fax or by mail.

COLORADO

BOULDER COUNTY, COLORADO

Web site for information:

www.co.boulder.co.us/treas/tax_sale/tax_lien_sale.htm

Boulder county treasurer

Tax lien sale

Common Q & A's

I. PRIOR TO SALE DATE

Q: When is the Tax Lien Sale Auction list published?

A: The delinquent tax lien sale list is published four weeks prior to the tax lien sale for three consecutive weeks. The publication is the same list each time it is printed.

Q: Where is the list published?

A: The delinquent list is put out for a bid each year to the daily and weekly newspapers within Boulder County. The paper winning the bid will publish the insert for the three consecutive weeks, four weeks prior to the sale. The list will then be published in the other papers once during the four week period.

Q: Are copies of the list available in the Treasurer's office?

A: Copies of the list are available in our office beginning on the first day of publication.

Q: Can copies be mailed? Is there a mailing list?

A: Copies of the insert may be mailed; our office requests that you send $1 to cover mailing cost. You may also send your dollar with your name and address any time during the year and be placed on our tax lien sale mailing list.

Q: Where is the sale held?

A: The sale is held at the Boulder County Court House at 13th and Pearl St., in the City of Boulder, on the third floor in the County Commissioner's hearing room.

Q: Is parking available to participants?

A: Parking is on your own. There are three city parking lots within three blocks of the Courthouse, there is a charge for parking in these lots. (NW corner of Broadway and Spruce St., RTD Complex at 14th and Walnut, and SE corner of Pearl and 15th.)

Q: Has the Treasurer's office researched any of the properties on the list?

A: The Boulder County Treasurer makes no warranties or representations on any property listed in the publication. The Treasurer does not, nor is allowed to, make inspections of these properties.

Q: How do I find out where properties are located?

A: The Boulder County Assessor's Office has parcel maps available for public use on the second floor of the Boulder County Court House at 13th and Pearl St. Additional information may be researched at the Clerk & Recorder's Office—Recording Division located at 1750 33rd St., Boulder, CO 80301.

Q: How do I update my list for properties that a lien will not be sold against?

A: As property owners pay their delinquent taxes prior to the tax lien sale, their accounts are crossed off the Treasurer's copy of the publication. This crossed-off list is available at the Treasurer's Office for public use. Additional copies are NOT available to be taken out of the Treasurer's Office.

Q: Do I get ownership to the property?

A: NO. You as a tax lien investor have no right, title, or interest to the property. You have only purchased a lien against the property based on delinquent taxes.

Q: Do I have any right to go on or inspect the properties I am interested in?

A: No. As in the previous question, you are only purchasing a lien. The owner of the property retains all rights of ownership, title, and privacy.

Q: Can I just come and observe the tax sale?

A: Yes, but please keep in mind that seating is limited. If the room is full, it would be appreciated if you would give up a seat to a registered participant and observe from the back of the room or outer corridor (speakers are set up for outside the hearing room).

Q: How early can I register for the sale?

A: You may preregister for the sale and have your named entered as a buyer beginning one week prior to the sale. Please keep in mind you will still have to pick up your auction number card and day-of-sale auction list the morning of the sale.

II. THE DAY OF SALE

1. REGISTRATION

Q: What time does registration begin?

A: The Treasurer's Office opens at 7:45 AM the day of the sale for registration of buyers.

Q: What types of funds will be accepted?

A: All deposits must be made in cash, certified check, bank cashier's check, or funds may also be wired. (Please contact the accounting department for wiring instructions.) Final determination regarding the acceptability of any deposit other than cash will be at the discretion of the Treasurer or his deputies.

Q: How much money do I have to put on deposit?

A: You must have the funds on deposit in the amount you wish to invest. I.e., you bid on a $1,000 tax lien, you make a $35 premium bid, then you must have $1,035 on deposit to succeed as the purchaser of that lien.

Q: What information will I need to have to register?

A: The registration form will include: name, address (where you want checks correspondence mailed), Social Security or Tax ID number for reporting to IRS. You will have to complete and sign a W-9 form to register.

Q: How will names appear on the records of the tax lien certificates?

A: The names on the Tax Lien Sale Certificates of Purchase will appear and be issued exactly as on your registration form. Please verify all spellings and wording on your registration form, as checks and deeds if applicable will be issued accordingly.

Q: How long will the sale last?

A: The sale will begin as close to 8:30 AM as possible and depending on the number of items to auction, may last until 5 PM. At that time, the Treasurer's staff will determine if the sale will be continued or adjourned to the next day. But in recent years, the sale has not gone past 3:00 PM.

Q: What is the interest rate?

A: The interest rate for 2006 was 15% per annum. The 2007 interest rate is not set yet.

Q: Will I earn interest for December on the liens I purchase?

A: Yes, you will earn at least one month of interest for December.

Q: How often is interest calculated?

A: Interest is calculated on a monthly basis, so if your lien is paid by the owner on the first day or last day of a month, you earn interest for the entire month.

2. THE AUCTION!

Q: Will there be an auctioneer?

A: Yes, Boulder County Treasurer has elected to have a professional auctioneer run the sale.

Q: Do you sell from the newspaper publication?

A: No. The sale will be conducted from the day-of-sale auction list. This list will be provided at the time of registration.

Q: Does the day-of-sale auction list follow the newspaper?

A: Yes, the day-of-sale auction list is printed in the same alphabetical order as the newspaper, but only contains the tax liens to be sold.

Q: How is the bidding done? (Rotation vs. Open)

A: Bidding is on an open and competitive basis. Everyone present with funds available may bid on any tax lien auctioned. Each item will be identified by a staff member. The auctioneer will then start the bidding process for the premium bid amount only. The final amount of the successful premium bid and the successful bidder number will be repeated by the auctioneer. Please keep in mind only the premium is being repeated, and that you have also paid the amount listed on the day-of-sale auction list.

Q: What is a premium?

A: Premium bids are the amounts over and above the taxes, interest, and fees listed on the day-of-sale list.

Q: Why is the competitive premium bid process used?

A: A competitive bidding process, that is open to everyone, is the best means of assuring a fair auction process.

Q: Is interest calculated on my premium bid?

A: No. You do not earn any interest on a premium bid. Your premium bid is the amount over and above the delinquent taxes you are willing to pay to buy that tax lien.

Q: Do I get my premium bid back?

A: No, as stated previously, you do not get your premium back. This is the amount you are paying to purchase the tax lien.

Q: What increments are premium bids in?

A: All premiums are in whole dollar amounts and increases are at the discretion of the auctioneer.

Q: What was the percent of premium bids from prior sales?

A: For the last five years, premium bids have ranged from 0–5 percent.

Q: Do all tax liens sold go for a premium?

A: Historically in Boulder County, the vast majority of tax liens have sold for a premium bid.

Q: How are premium bid monies used by county government?

A: Money collected as premium bids goes directly to the County general fund and is not earmarked for any specific department or program. No premium bid funds are retained by the Treasurer's Office.

Q: Can I lose money investing in tax lien sales?

A: Yes, there is the possibility of losing money if the interest earned does not equal or exceed the premium bid amount paid. Should the property go all the way through the deed process and you get title to the land, the market value of that parcel may not be worth what you have invested in it. This is a buyer beware process, and investors need to make informed bids.

Q: Why are several items grouped together on the day-of-sale auction list?

A: By statute, the Treasurer may combine properties that are under the same ownership and sell those items as a group. If you purchase a group of items, you will still receive individual tax lien certificates of purchase for each item. These items do not have to be redeemed as a group by the property owner. This practice is used solely to expedite the sale.

Q: In terms of other encumbrances, what position are the tax liens?

A: Tax liens are a first, prior, and perpetual lien against the property, meaning taxes are in a first position over mortgages, mechanic liens, and judgments. The only lien that would be ahead of a tax lien is a prior tax lien.

Q: What if I purchase a lien for more money than I have on deposit? How will I be notified I am out of funds during the sale?

A: If you bid and are successful in purchasing a lien on an item you do not have sufficient funds to cover, your buyer number will be printed on a board in the front of the room. At that time you must go directly to the conference room, located across the hall from the hearing room, and put additional money in your account. The item that you bid on is on hold and cannot be credited to your purchases until this additional deposit is made. If your number is put on the board, please do not continue bidding on additional items until you have replenished your funds. If funds are not available, the item will be resold prior to the end of the sale.

Q: Can I make additional deposits during the sale?

A: Yes, you can make additional deposits anytime throughout the sale in the conference room.

Q: When can I get an update of my purchases and account balance?

A: A buyer balance sheet is available anytime in the conference room. This sheet will tell you what you have on deposit, what you have purchased, and your account balance.

Q: How fast will the sale go?

A: The sale will proceed at a deliberate and steady pace. If at any time you feel you are getting lost or can not keep up with the pace of the sale, please contact the Treasurer or a staff member, and we will try to make adjustments that will be satisfactory to everyone.

Q: What if I bid and am the successful bidder on a lien in error?

A: The tax lien sale is a buyer beware situation, it is your responsibility to know what lien is being auctioned and how much you have bid. Once a lien is sold to you, unless you do not have funds to cover the purchase, we cannot reverse the sale.

III. AFTER THE AUCTION

Q: When can I get my refund of my deposit?

A: No refunds will be issued on the day of sale. Refunds of any monies left in buyers' accounts will be available to be picked up in the Treasurer's Office (1st floor, Boulder County Courthouse, 13th and Pearl St.) after 12 noon on the following Tuesday. If you choose not to pick up your refunds, checks will be mailed by request on the Wednesday following the sale. Any remaining checks will be mailed by the Friday following the sale. If funds are wired in, wires of refunds will be sent out the Tuesday following the sale.

Q: What is a Tax Lien Sale Certificate of Purchase?

A: A Tax Lien Sale Certificate of Purchase will be issued for each lien to the successful bidder. This statutory form will show the legal description, purchase amount, buyer's name (as entered from the registration card), interest rate, date of sale, owner of record, and mailing address as of advertising, as well as space provided for endorsement of subsequent year's taxes.

Q: Will I get the original Tax Lien Sale Certificates of Purchase?

A: No, Boulder County Treasurer is holding in safekeeping all Tax Lien Sale Certificates of Purchase. Copies of each certificate will be mailed to you with your refund checks, if applicable, or separately within a week following the sale.

Q: Will a printout be available of what I purchased?

A: Yes, if you choose to come in and pick up your refund check you will be asked to sign for the refund, and on that sheet is a complete list of all purchases you made at the sale. We can also send a copy of this list upon your request.

Q: May I sell the Tax Lien Sale Certificates of Purchase to another party?

A: Yes, tax lien certificates are assignable to another party. On the back side of each original certificate of purchase, there is a place for the assignment of your interest. Because the Treasurer's Office holds your certificates, you will need to contact the Treasurer's Office to assign your certificate(s). All certificates must be notarized and have signatures from everyone whose name appears on the certificates. Each certificate that has been assigned must be recorded with the Boulder County Clerk and Recorder (there is a charge for recording each certificate, currently $11 each). Also, the Treasurer's Office will need the party to whom you are assigning your certificate to complete a W-9 reporting form.

Q: What is an endorsement of subsequent taxes?

A: Each year following the purchase of your original certificate, if the property owner has not paid their current year taxes in the timely manner required by statute, you have the option of adding that next year's delinquent taxes to your certificate.

Q: Do I have to pay subsequent taxes each year?

A: No, you as the tax sale purchaser may determine whether or not you want to pay any additional taxes by endorsement.

Q: Will I be notified of subsequent endorsement amounts I need to pay?

A: Yes, the Treasurer's Office will send out a computer print of what certificates may be endorsed and the amount to endorse each of those certificates.

Q: Do I have to pay a premium on endorsement amounts?

A: No, once you have purchased the original tax lien, the endorsement amount is the next year's delinquent tax plus interest due at time of delinquency and endorsement fee (currently $5).

Q: When can I pay subsequent taxes?

A: Subsequent delinquent taxes may be endorsed anytime after July 1 of any given year.

Q: What interest rate will I earn on endorsement amounts?

A: The interest rate is set at the original sale and remains the same for the life of the lien.

Q: Do property owners contact me to cure tax lien?

A: No, all tax lien sale redemption must be made through the Treasurer's Office.

Q: How soon can tax liens be paid off by the property owners?

A: The Treasurer's Office will begin accepting redemptions from property owners for the 2006 sale on Wednesday, December 6, 2006.

Q: What percent of the tax liens get paid off within the first year?

A: Due to the high number of factors that could be figured into a statistic like this, it is difficult to give an average figure.

Q: How many properties go all the way to a Treasurer's Deed?

A: Less then one-half of one percent go to tax deed.

Q: When can I apply for a Treasurer's Deed?

A: Three years from the date of the original tax lien sale you can request that the Treasurer's Office start the deed procedures.

Q: What kind of title does a Treasurer's Deed give?

A: A Treasurer's Deed transfers ownership free and clear of all liens. This title is not a warrantable title for up to nine years from the date of deed.

Q: What happens to a tax lien if the property owner files bankruptcy?

A: When a bankruptcy is filed and it effects property in Boulder County, the Treasurer's Office receives notice and files a proof of claim with the Bankruptcy Court. Our proof of claim includes the tax lien sale interest rate. To date we have not been denied our full claim on tax sale liens. Your tax lien continues to earn interest, but the bankruptcy does prevent the issuing of a Treasurer's Deed until the bankruptcy has been dismissed. In the unlikely event that the Bankruptcy Court does not comply with our request, the Boulder County Treasurer would take all available action to cure your lien.

Q: Do you pay interest in annual payments?

A: No, interest is only paid when the tax lien is redeemed.

Q: What will be reported to the IRS?

A: In 1994 the law was changed to require County Treasurers to report interest earned by investors on tax lien sales. Once a year our office reports on 1099 interest earning statements to the IRS. The amount reported is the total interest paid from each redeemed certificate during that year. A 1099 statement will be sent to each buyer in January. The interest is reported from redemption date, not check date. (I.e., a certificate is redeemed on December 29, 2006, and your check is issued on January 2, 2007, then the interest will be reported with your 2006 statement.)

Q: Can I claim premium bids as an expense/cost on my income tax?

A: We are prohibited by law from giving legal advice or tax advice to individuals. You will need to contact your accountant or a member of the Internal Revenue Service.

FLORIDA

ORANGE COUNTY, FLORIDA
Web sites for information:
www.octaxcol.com/TaxeSale/TaxSale.htm
www.octaxcol.com/TaxeSale/TaxSaleProcedure.htm
Earl K. Wood
Orange County Tax Collector
200 South Orange Avenue, Suite 1500
Orlando, Florida 32801
(407) 836-2700

Orange County Tax Certificate Sale, 2006

The annual Tax Certificate Sale for prior year delinquent taxes will be held via the Internet from Wednesday, May 31, 2006. The sale will start at 9:00 AM and will run until approximately 4:00 PM.

Please visit the Orange County Tax Collector's bidding site *www.bidorangecounty.com* for details. Although you may register any time from May 15, 2006 through the end of the sale, you are advised to register and bid well in advance of the sale date, since the sale will proceed at a fast pace. All deposits and payments will be made by electronic funds transfer. Bidders are required to complete a W-9 form. The information obtained from the W-9 form will be reported to the IRS on the year-end 1099-INT statement.

The delinquent list will be published three consecutive Mondays beginning May 15, 2006, by the *Orlando Sentinel*. The other dates are May 22 and May 29, 2006. On May 15, 2006, the delinquent accounts will be posted to the Tax Collector's Web site *www.octaxcol.com* and to the *www.bidorangecounty.com* site. The delinquent information will be updated periodically until the sale.

Not all of the items printed in the newspaper will be sold, due to late payments received after the list was prepared for publication. Revenue from the sale pay for the ad valorem property taxes/non ad valorem assessments, interest, and costs and charges related to the sale.

A deposit of 10 percent of the amount a bidder expects to purchase is required. If the bidder exceeds that amount during the sale, further bidding will not be permitted until additional funds are deposited.

There will be computers with bid site access available at the Tax Collector's Office for those bidders without other access to computers. Use of these computers will be by appointment only. Please call (407) 836-2778 to schedule a session.

The advertising list will include the amount of taxes due, as well as interest and the cost of the sale, which represents the face value of the tax certificate. Simple interest for the amount that the certificate was purchased will be calculated. Any bidder has the right to bid on any certificate, as long as the deposit requirement is met. Tax certificates are sold in the order they appear on the tax roll.

The bidder willing to accept the lowest interest rate is awarded the certificate. If there are no bidders for a certificate, it will be struck to the County. Bidding starts at 18 percent and interest is bid down until there are no lower offers. "No Interest" bids will give the bidder the certificate at 0 percent interest. *Per F.S. 197.472 (2), the mandatory charge of 5 percent does not apply to any interest rate bid of 0 percent. Bids of 0 percent will earn 0 interest.* Bids shall be accepted in even and fractional increments of quarter-percent points only.

Certificates will be issued in the name of a person or a corporation. After the sale, certificates may be sold and transferred by assignment through the Delinquent Tax Department. A fee of $2.50 is charged for each certificate transferred. When making inquiries about tax certificates or when requesting an address change, please provide the delinquent tax department with all Social Security numbers/Federal Tax ID numbers currently and previously used to buy certificates.

The sale will continue until delivery of all certificates. If a bidder fails to pay for certificates, the deposit will be forfeited and the certificates will be resold by the Tax Collector. Any bidder in default will be barred from future tax certificate sales in Orange County.

Bidders will be notified of certificates purchased and the balance due within 24 hours of the closing of the Internet auction. Balance of payment will be required within 48 hours of email notification. If you do not receive a bill, please contact our tax office immediately at (407) 836-2778.

Upon redemption of tax certificates, interest shall be calculated on a monthly basis from the first day of each month beginning June 1. Certificate holders shall draw no interest during April and May while the mandatory charge is in effect (FS 197.172). Application for tax deed may be made no sooner than two years after the delinquency date, April 1.

The holder of a tax certificate may not directly, through an agent, or otherwise initiate contact with the owner of property for which he or she holds a tax certificate to encourage or demand payment until two years have elapsed since April 1 of the year of issuance of the tax certificate—FS 197.432 (14) anyone taking action prior to two years after April 1, may be barred from bidding at a Tax Certificate Sale by Tax Collector and held actionable under applicable law prohibiting fraud S 501.204.

Caution: You are hereby informed that this is not a sale of land, but a lien for the amount of delinquent taxes plus interest. Certificates issued will be in effect for a period of seven years, and then canceled by *Act of the 1973 Florida Legislature.* Purchasing a tax certificate does not entitle the certificate buyer to enter the property, nor harass the owner in any manner.

Certificate value may be affected by subsequently filed bankruptcy cases.

There is risk to principal and interest with respect to tax certificates if property conditions or the utility changes. This is true when changes are made to correct errors arising from obvious or concealed facts. The Property Appraiser may correct only *clerical* errors after the tax roll has been certified (Markham v. Friedland, 245 So. 2d 645 Fla. 1971/ Korash v. Mills, 263 So. 2d 579 [Fla. 1972]).

In a few recent instances, principal and interest were lost to Orange County certificate holders when the land changed from undeveloped status to ineligible for development (e.g., wetlands). **Certificates issued prior to the change lost value.** Bidders are cautioned to select carefully the parcels bid upon to minimize risk of loss. Timeshare and subsurface parcels will *not* be specifically identified before the certificate is sold.

Procedures for 2006 Tax Certificate Sale of 2005 Real Properties in Orange County, Florida

Authorization: Florida Statute 197.432 (16)

The sale shall be in compliance with the procedures provided in the referenced chapter.

Advertising Dates: May 15, May 22, and May 29, 2006, published in the *Orlando Sentinel* newspaper.

Location: Internet site *www.bidorangecounty.com.*

Site developed and conducted by Grant Street Group, parent of MuniAuction.

Sale Date: May 31, 2006; time: 9:00 AM until 4:00 PM each day until all certificates are issued.

ON-LINE REGISTRATION

- IRS form W-9 required for each Social Security number. Only one bidding number per Social Security number is allowed.
- Foreign buyers: IRS Form W-7 required to be submitted to IRS for each ITIN number. Only one bidding number per ITIN number will be allowed.
- Deposits need to be submitted on Web site electronically (ACH) in U.S. funds from a U.S. banking institution.

BIDDING PROCESS

- Must be registered (*www.bidorangecounty.com*).
- Deposit of 10 percent of amount expected to spend is required. When you reach your limit, additional deposit is required in order to continue.

- Lowest rate of interest bid will be awarded the tax certificate. Interest starts at 18 percent and is bid down to 0 percent. *Per F.S.197.472 (2), the mandatory charge of 5 percent does not apply to any interest rate bid of 0 percent. Bids of 0 percent will earn 0 interest.* Bids shall be accepted in even and fractional increments of quarter-percentage points.
- Certificates will be sold in sequential order as they appear in the newspaper. The face amount of each certificate is equal to the gross tax, interest, advertising, and the cost of the sale.
- Registered bidders will be able to compile their list of items and percentage amount on May 15, 2006, up until the day of the sale, May 31, 2006.
- The auction will consist of batches of approximately 1000 items. Each batch commences at 9:00 AM on May 31, 2006 and continues hourly until the close of the sale.

CLOSE OF SALE

- Upon the completion of the Tax Certificate Sale, the Tax Collector's Office will reconcile the accounts with Grant Street Group. Bidders will then be notified of certificates purchased. The tax certificate will be issued to the party as registered on the Web site (Registration Page).
- Final payment is due electronically (ACH) via the Web site upon completion of reconciliation—48 hours upon sale completion.

NOTICE

At the conclusion of each batch, bidders will be able to get an unofficial total of their purchases. The official notice will be provided by the Tax Collector's Office via mail.

This is not a sale of land, but a lien for the amount of delinquent taxes.

Any holder of a tax certificate who, prior to the date two years after April 1 of the year of issuance of the tax certificate, initiates, or whose agent initiates, contact with the property owner upon which he or she holds a certificate encouraging or demanding payment may be barred by the Tax Collector from bidding at a Tax Certificate Sale. (F.S. 197.432 (15))

CAUTION TO CERTIFICATE BUYERS

There are risks involved with buying certificates, and those risks are borne solely by the certificate holder.

PALM BEACH COUNTY, FLORIDA

Web site for information:

www.pbcgov.com/tax/ServicesProvided/Tax_Sale/Tax%20Certificate%20Sale.htm

Tax Collector, Palm Beach County

2006 Tax Certificate Sale

1. The Tax Certificate Sale of unpaid 2005 real property taxes will begin at 8:30 AM, June 1, 2006. The sale will be conducted on the Palm Beach County Tax Collector's tax certificate auction Web site, *www.BidPBTC.com*. Computer terminals are available for public use at 301 N. Olive Ave., West Palm Beach, Palm Beach County, Florida, by appointment. To schedule an appointment, please call (561) 355-3546. In the event that the sale can not be held on the auction Web site, a live auction will be held at the time and location listed above.

2. To be eligible to bid, you must complete the following steps on *www.bidpbtc.com*:

- Complete online registration.
- Complete IRS Form W-9.
- Submit a deposit (online via ACH).
- Establish a budget.
- Receive bidder number assignment.

A Social Security number or Tax Identification number must be provided for each buyer and must belong to the person

listed on the W-9 form. There will be only one bidder number assigned to each Social Security number or Tax ID number. The tax certificate list, redemption checks, and 1099 interest earnings will be issued exactly as indicated on your W-9 form. **Until the tax sale is complete, no changes will be made to the bidder number issued. A change of name or Tax Identification number will constitute an assignment and is subject to service charge for each certificate changed.**

3. A deposit of 10 pecent of your expected bids must be made prior to the close of any batch in which you intend to submit bids. All payments must be made via the Payments Page on the BidPBTC.com Web site. Payments will not be accepted via any other means. There will be no exceptions to these requirements.

4. Bidding starts at 18 percent and interest is bid down until sold. Bids may be made in quarter-percent increments. A "zero" interest bid will get the bidder the certificate with NO interest. When your bid is recognized as the low bid on the Results Page, you are obligated to pay for the certificate even if the bid was unintentional.

5. The properties will be auctioned in the order listed in the newspaper. The delinquent taxes from prior years will be auctioned first. After the prior years are posted, the 2005 delinquent taxes will be posted. Bidders will be able to begin entering interest rates on the Web site beginning the day that the first newspaper advertisement is published. Some items listed in the newspaper and on the Web site will not be auctioned due to payments being received after the list was prepared for publication. Certificates will be sold individually and will be divided into eight batches each day, available for sale each hour on the half hour. Batches will close starting at 8:30 AM to 3:30 PM EDT daily until all certificates are sold.

6. The payment balance for certificates purchased must be made within 48 hours from the postmark on your notice of amount due. A certificate of ownership and listing of certificates purchased is provided to each buyer. A bidder failing to make payment in the specified time will forfeit the deposit, and the certificates will be resold.

7. The Tax Collector reserves the right to cancel or correct certificates issued in error. Interest payments may be affected by bankruptcies, U.S. Marshal seizures, property taken over by a receiver, etc.
8. Caution: This is not a sale of real property. It is a lien for the amount of delinquent taxes plus interest. Contact with property owners initiated by certificate owners to encourage payment at any time is not recommended. Contact or behavior of a certificate holder deemed unfair or deceptive may result in criminal prosecution. A tax deed application is the proper and legal method to compel payment.

We in the Tax Collector's Office are happy to be of service to you. We are available to assist you as needed.

–Anne M. Gannon, Tax Collector

Delinquent Real Estate Taxes & Tax Certificate Sale Frequently Asked Questions (Modified 1/3/05)

This information has been compiled to answer the most frequently asked questions about delinquent real estate taxes and the sale of tax certificates on the Internet. Although the facts and procedures provided in the answers are based on Florida law, the administration of delinquent real estate taxes by the office of the Palm Beach County Tax Collector has two basic objectives:

1. to collect the maximum amount of delinquent taxes for the taxing bodies, while
2. protecting the interest of the property owner who, for some reason, did not pay the taxes due.

WHEN ARE REAL ESTATE TAXES AND NON–AD VALOREM ASSESSMENTS DUE IN FLORIDA?

Real Estate taxes and non–ad valorem assessments are due each calendar year and are payable November 1 (or later if the tax roll is not certified by the Property Appraiser early enough to meet that date). The taxes become delinquent April 1 of the following year.

WHAT HAPPENS WHEN REAL ESTATE TAXES AND NON–AD VALOREM ASSESSMENTS BECOME DELINQUENT?

Three percent interest (18 percent per annum for two months) plus advertising cost is added when payment is made in April or May. The Tax Collector is required to conduct a sale of tax certificates to collect the preceding year's unpaid real estate taxes. The sale must start on or before June 1, unless a late tax roll makes this impossible.

ARE DELINQUENT TAXES PUBLICIZED?

The Tax Collector must advertise the delinquent taxes in a general circulation newspaper. The Board of County Commissioners chooses the newspaper. The advertisement is printed weekly, three times prior to the Tax Certificate Sale.

WHAT DOES THE NEWSPAPER AD CONTAIN?

The place, date, and time of the tax certificate sale. A listing of each parcel showing the delinquent tax amount, the property owner's name, and the property control number. The parcels are consecutively numbered for reference during the sale. The delinquent tax amount (certificate's face amount) consists of the sum of the following: real estate tax and non–ad valorem assessment amount, interest (4.5 percent for months of April, May, and June), Tax Collector commission (5 percent), newspaper and Internet advertising charges, and a fee for the cost associated with the sale of tax certificates on the Internet.

WHAT ARE "TAX CERTIFICATES"?

They are a first lien on the real estate. Buyers are provided a certificate of ownership and a listing of all certificates purchased.

HOW DOES SOMEONE ACQUIRE A TAX CERTIFICATE?

At the public auction conducted on June 1 of each year. The auction is called a Tax Certificate Sale.

WHO MAY PARTICIPATE IN THE TAX CERTIFICATE SALE?

Anyone. To participate in the sale a bidder must register with the Tax Collector's office via the BidPBTC.com Web site. A bidder number is assigned for identification purposes during the sale. Bidders are required to make a deposit via ACH Debit on the BidPBTC.com Payments Page that is 10 percent of the estimated amount they intend to purchase. The deposit may be increased any time prior to the close of the auction.

WHAT DO I DO IF I FORGET MY PASSWORD?

Please be careful to remember your password, as it is the key to your access to the BidPBTC.com Web site. If, however, you forget your password, it may be recovered easily by clicking on the "Forgot your password?" link on the BidPBTC.com home page. When you provide your matching personal information, a new temporary password will be sent to your registered email address. This password will need to be changed after your next log-in.

WHAT IS AN INTERNET AUCTION?

An auction in which bids are transmitted and received through the Internet using a computer and a Web browser.

HOW DOES THE BIDDING PROCEED?

Each item is auctioned in the order listed in the publication. The bidding begins at 18 percent (the maximum rate) and is bid down. The "winning" bidder's number and rate of interest are recorded. Any item not bid upon is "sold" to the County.

WHEN ARE MY BIDS DUE?

Bids can be submitted on the Web site once the Advertised List is published on the Internet, usually in early May. The advertised list will be divided into 24 batches. Bids can be withdrawn or altered at any point up to the closing of the Batch on the day of the sale.

WHAT EQUIPMENT OR SOFTWARE DO I NEED TO BE ABLE TO PARTICIPATE?

A bidder must have a computer with Internet access and a Web browser (recommended: Internet Explorer 5.0 or higher on Windows 98, Me, NT, 2000, or XP; Netscape 7.1 or higher; Mozilla Firefox 0.8 or higher). If you do not have access to a computer, the Tax Collector will supply computers for training and/or bidding by appointment. You can reach the Tax Collector's Office at (561) 355-3546.

WHO WILL SHOW ME HOW TO USE THE INTERNET AUCTION SYSTEM?

Users are encouraged to participate in a Self-Demo, Trial Auction, or a Guided Demo prior to bidding.

- Self-Demo: Please click the Demo button on the home page and follow the instructions. The instructions are designed to lead users through the auction process.
- Trial Auction: Please click the Trial Auction button on the home page. The Trial Auction is a simulation of a real auction, in which bidders practice bidding and, subsequently, view auction results.
- Guided Demo: Please contact Auction Support to receive a Guided Demo (which is available only after user completes the Self-Demo). Auction Support will guide the user through the auction process on the Web site over the phone at (800) 410-3445, x1.

WHAT IS A BATCH?

A batch is an auction subgroup of the Advertised List that serves as a means of organizing tax certificates for the purpose of facilitating bid submission. Each tax certificate in each batch is auctioned independently of every other tax certificate and arranged in sequential order with a unique auction closing time for each batch.

WHAT IS PROXY BIDDING?

In a live auction, a bidder will lower his bid by quarter-percent increments until he is the only bidder left or until the interest goes below his acceptable minimum level, at which point he would drop out. Proxy bidding is a form of competitive sale in which bidders enter the minimum interest rate that they are willing to accept for each certificate. The auction system acts as an electronic agent, submitting bids on behalf of each bidder. The result of the proxy system is that the electronic agent keeps lowering the bid to submit by quarter-percent increments until you are either the only bidder left (in which case you get the certificate at a quarter-percent lower than the previous bid), or until you reach the floor you have set. Zero percent bids will not be treated as proxy bids. They will be awarded at zero.

If you are the only bidder on a given certificate and your minimum rate is greater than 0 percent, the electronic agent will submit a bid of 18 percent on your behalf.

In the case of a tie at the winning bid rate, the system awards to one of the tie bidders through a random selection process using a random number generator.

In no case will a bidder be awarded a certificate at a rate lower than his specified minimum acceptable rate.

Certificates that receive no bids will be struck to the county at 18 percent.

WHEN DO THE BIDDERS HAVE TO PAY THE AMOUNT DUE FOR THEIR PURCHASE?

After the sale they are given a certain date by which they must pay the balance due via ACH Debit on the Payments Page of the BidPBTC.com Web site. Failure to pay by that date results in the forfeiture of the deposit and makes the certificates available for resale.

WHAT IS AN ACH DEBIT?

An ACH debit is an electronic funds transfer from your bank account, initiated by the Tax Collector with your prior authorization. Debits entered on the Payments Page of the Web site will be submitted immediately for processing.

Funds must be drawn from a U.S. financial institution. Some types of money market, brokerage, and/or trust accounts cannot accept ACH debits. Please check with your financial institution prior to initiating payment on the Web site.

For more information on ACH, please visit the NACHA, the Electronic Payments Association, at *www.nacha.org*.

WHAT HAPPENS TO MY DEPOSIT IF I DON'T WIN ANY CERTIFICATES IN THE AUCTION?

Refunds for unused portions of the deposit will be issued via ACH debit by the Tax Collector to your bank account.

HOW DOES THE HOLDER OF THE CERTIFICATE RECEIVE THE INTEREST INCOME?

The Tax Collector remits the principal (face amount of certificate) and the interest earnings when the property taxes are eventually paid or when a Tax Deed is executed.

CAN INTEREST RATES BE CHANGED AFTER THE BID?

When a certificate is redeemed and the interest earned is less than 5 percent, a mandatory charge of 5 percent is due. This applies to all certificates except those with an interest rate bid of 0 percent. If a certificate should be cancelled or reduced, the interest earned will be 8 percent per year, simple interest or the rate of interest bid at the tax certificate sale, whichever is less on the cancelled or reduced amount. Bankruptcy rulings may also affect interest rates.

WHY WOULD A CERTIFICATE BE CANCELLED OR REDUCED?

To correct errors, omissions, or double assessments and when ordered by a court.

ARE TAX SALE CERTIFICATES TRANSFERABLE?

Certificates may be transferred by completing an endorsement form and paying the applicable fees.

WHAT ABOUT TAX CERTIFICATES ISSUED TO THE COUNTY?

County-held tax certificates, other than those on homestead real estate under $100, may be acquired by individuals after the close of the tax sale. The Tax Collector will announce the date(s) these certificates become available.

WHAT IS THE "LIFE" OF A TAX CERTIFICATE?

Certificates are dated as of the first day of the sale and are null and void seven years from the date of issuance. When two years have elapsed since April 1 of the year of issuance, the holder of a tax certificate may submit a Tax Deed Application to the Tax Collector.

WHAT IS THE TAX DEED PROCESS?

Any certificate holder, other than the county, making application for a Tax Deed, must pay the Tax Collector a title search fee, an application fee, and the amount required for redemption of all other outstanding tax certificates, interest, omitted taxes, and current taxes. The executed application forces the sale of the property at public auction.

CAN HOMESTEAD PROPERTY BE SOLD BY TAX DEED?

Yes, but the opening bid must be increased by one-half of the assessed value of the property.

WHO CONDUCTS THE TAX DEED SALE?

The Clerk of the Circuit Court. The Tax Deed is issued to the highest bidder. The opening bid must cover all the costs paid by the Tax Deed applicant plus all other costs for conducting the sale. The title-holder of record has the right to redeem the property, prior to the issuance of a Tax Deed, by paying the Tax Collector all previously described costs.

Anne M. Gannon
Tax Collector
Palm Beach County
301 North Olive Avenue
West Palm Beach, Florida 33401

In accordance with the provisions of ADA, this document may be requested in an alternate format.
Contact the Tax Collector's Office at (561) 355-2269.

NOTICE

The offer or sale of vacant residential lots or parcels in a subdivision may be subject to the Land Sales Practices requirements of Chapter 498, Florida Statutes, and may require you to be registered with Florida Department of Business and Professional Regulation, Division of Florida Land Sales, Condominiums, and Mobile Homes. As a point of information, an individual (who is not a developer is allowed to buy a Tax Deed for only one lot in a planned subdivision for the purpose of resale. Section 498.025(1), Florida Statutes states: The provisions of this chapter do not apply to: the offer or disposition of an interest in subdivided lands by a purchaser for his or her own account in a single isolated transaction. The Bureau of Florida Land Sales has stated that its concerns are with providing disclosure to persons who are successful bidders; and who after two years apply for a tax deed, and who at the courthouse public auction obtain multiple Tax Deeds, for the purpose of resale to multiple purchasers. A seller of lots in property subdivided or proposed to be subdivided into 50 lots or more is required to be registered with the Department of Business and Professional Regulation, Division of Florida Land Sales, Condominiums, and Mobile Homes. Also, if a certificate holder purchases five certificates in a subdivision that contains 25 or more lots, and eventually obtained five Tax Deeds, he would be subject to the provisions of section 498.022, Florida Statutes, regarding standards for transacting land sales. Therefore, it is recommended that, when purchasing certificates on lots or parcels in a subdivision, the Department of Business and Professional Regulation, Division of Florida Land Sales, Condominiums, and Mobile Homes be contacted at (850) 488-1631 to ascertain your responsibility with regard to subsequent sales transactions of lots in that subdivision.

IOWA

BLACK HAWK COUNTY, IOWA

Web site for information:
www.co.black-hawk.ia.us/depts/treasurer.html

2007 TAX SALE

The annual Black Hawk County Tax Sale will be held Monday, June 18, 2007, in Courtroom #301 at the address listed above. The sale will begin at 8:30 AM and end at 3:30 PM each day until all delinquent taxes have been offered for sale. Any Regular Tax Sale delinquencies that are offered at the Annual Tax Sale but remain unsold will be offered at an Adjourned Tax Sale which will be held the third Monday of each month until all delinquencies have been sold in the Treasurer's Office, Room #140 of the Courthouse, beginning at 8:30 AM.

The bidder registration and IRS W-9 form, with original signatures, must be completed and received by the Treasurer's Office by noon, Friday, June 15, 2007. A $40 per bidder registration fee must accompany the registration documents.

All delinquencies as of May 1, 2007, will be published in the *Waterloo/Cedar Falls Courier* on or about June 7, 2007. Periodic updates of the delinquencies along with the bidder registration documents and tax sale terms and conditions can be found at *www.co.black-hawk.ia.us*, Treasurer's Department.

Should any additional information be required, please do not hesitate to contact the Treasurer's Office at (319) 833-3013.

TERMS AND CONDITIONS GOVERNING THE ANNUAL TAX SALE OF JUNE 18, 2007, AND ADJOURNMENTS OR ASSIGNMENTS THEREOF:

1. BIDDER REGISTRATION

Each bidder must properly complete the following forms:
  a. Bidder Registration Form
  b. IRS W-9 Form
  c. Agent Authorization Form

All bidders, designated representatives, and assignees must be 18 years of age as of June 18, 2007. Valid proof of age will be required.

All registered bidders will be issued a numbered bidder card prior to the commencement of the Annual Tax Sale. Bidders may call for their cards in the Treasurer's Office at 8:00 AM, Monday, June 18, 2007.

2. ELECTRONIC DEVICES PROHIBITED

Cellular phones, pagers, tape recorders, camcorders, and other audible electronic devices are to be turned off during the sale. Laptop or notebook computers are allowed only if they are operated from battery packs.

3. BIDDING

All properties with one year, or less, of delinquent taxes and/or special assessments will have those delinquencies plus interest, fees, and costs, offered for sale at the Regular Tax Sale in parcel number order. Real estate delinquencies will be offered first with mobile home delinquencies to follow.

All delinquent taxes and/or special assessments that have been previously offered for one year and remain unsold for want of bidders will be offered at the Public Bidder Tax Sale in parcel order number. Real estate delinquencies will be offered first with mobile home delinquencies to follow. Should there be no private sector bid, the Treasurer is required to purchase the Public Bidder Tax Sale delinquencies on behalf of the County.

All delinquent taxes and/or special assessments upon property for which a city within Black Hawk County has declared by affidavit to be abandoned or a public nuisance shall be offered at the Public Nuisance Tax Sale. The delinquencies will be sold to the certifying city. In order for a private buyer to bid at the Public Nuisance Tax Sale, a rehabilitation agreement with the city must be in place and a copy of this agreement provided to the Treasurer's Office by noon, Friday, June 15, 2007.

Tax sale delinquencies must be sold for the exact amount of delinquent taxes and/or special assessments plus interest, fees, and costs. In no case will a lesser or greater bid amount be accepted. Should there be more than one person interested in purchasing the taxes for the same property, the bid for the lesser interest in the property will be the successful bid. For example, when two people are interested in purchasing delinquent taxes in the amount of $1,000 for the same property, the bid must be exactly $1,000 but the bidder may take an 80 percent interest in the property rather than a 100 percent interest for that amount. Further, if two or more bidders have placed an equal bid and the bids are the smallest percentage offered, with a minimum of 1 percent acceptable, the Treasurer will use a random selection process to determine the successful bidder.

Upon entering the Courtroom, bidders are asked to seat themselves in numerical order by bidder number, beginning at the right front of the room. Each parcel will be announced by item number, in parcel number order. To bid, the bidder card must be raised above head level so that it can be readily seen by those conducting the tax sale. One person may bid for multiple private buyers at tax sale but may hold only one bidder card; i.e., private buyer "A" registers ten bidders, each having an individual Social Security or federal identification number. Private buyer "A" will receive one bidder card having ten bidder numbers listed for the ten registered bidders.

If more than one bidder is interested in purchasing the delinquent taxes for the same property, the bid down of interest is to be made verbally in increments of 10 percent, and then increments of 1 percent when 10 percent has been reached. One percent is the minimum acceptable bid. If the bid down of interest has reached a stalemate, a random selection process will be used to determine the successful bidder. The bidder selected by the random selection process must promptly accept by verbally indicating "sold," or refuse by saying "pass." Failure to immediately respond or to not respond at a volume level that can be heard by those conducting the sale will be considered a "pass," and the random selection process will be run again to select another bidder. The color coding of the random selection process is: white background with black foreground, active bidder; white background with red foreground, deactivated bidder; black background with white foreground, selected as successful bidder; white background with blue foreground, passed after being selected as successful bidder.

4. PURCHASE OF TAX SALE CERTIFICATES

At the close of each day's sale, or upon a bidder's purchase completion, a report of each private buyer's purchases will be printed in the Treasurer's Office. Please provide the staff at Cashier Window #1 in the Treasurer's Office on first floor with your bidder card to facilitate the report process. The private buyer is required to reconcile the County report with his or her records, and upon reconciliation, sign, date, and return the report to the Treasurer's staff at Window #1. One copy of the signed report will be retained by the Treasurer's Office; the second copy will be given to the private buyer at tax sale. Failure to return a signed report each day of participation will cause the previously purchased delinquencies to be re-offered for sale. Any discrepancies are to be immediately researched and resolved.

Full payment is due at the close of the tax sale or upon a bidder's purchase completion. The amount collected will include all delinquent taxes, special assessments, interest, fees, costs, and a $20 certificate fee for each Certificate of Purchase at Tax Sale issued. Payment must be made in U.S. funds and in the form of a personal or business check, money order, or any form of guaranteed funds for the exact amount of the purchase.

If a tax sale buyer's check fails to be honored by the bank upon which it is drawn, the buyer will have five business days following notification by the Treasurer's Office to repay with guaranteed funds, or the Certificates of Purchase at Tax Sale will be canceled. A $30 service fee will be collected for each dishonored check.

If a wire transfer is requested as the payment method, instructions will be provided at Cashier Window #1. The wire transfer funds must be received by 2:00 PM central time on the day following the final purchase at tax sale.

5. CERTIFICATE OF PURCHASE AT TAX SALE

A Certificate of Purchase at Tax Sale will be issued to the successful bidder. The Certificate will be mailed to the private buyer by the Treasurer's Office as soon as possible following conclusion of the tax sale.

Should an original Certificate of Purchase at Tax Sale be lost or destroyed, the private buyer must notify the Treasurer's Office, which will prepare an Affidavit of Loss to be completed by the private buyer. The Treasurer's Office will prepare a replacement Certificate of Purchase at Tax Sale for a fee of $20 per replacement Certificate.

6. ASSIGNMENT OF THE CERTIFICATE OF PURCHASE AT TAX SALE

The Certificate of Purchase at Tax Sale, whether held by a private buyer or the County, is assignable by endorsement of the Certificate and entry in the Treasurer's Tax Sale Register. For each private buyer to private buyer assignment transaction, the Treasurer charges the assignee a fee of $100, or $10 in the case of an assignment by an estate. The fee for a County to private buyer assignment is $10 per parcel. The assignment transaction fee is not added to the amount necessary to redeem. A copy of the Certificate of Purchase at Tax Sale with an original signature endorsement should be forwarded to the Treasurer's Office along with the appropriate fee in order to properly accomplish an assignment.

No trading of parcels between private buyers will be allowed. An official assignment of a Certificate of Purchase at Tax Sale is required.

7. SUBSEQUENT TAXES AND/OR SPECIAL ASSESSMENTS

Because each tax year stands on its own, a tax bill for the 2007–2008 taxes and special assessments will be mailed in August to the person in whose name the parcel is taxed. In addition, a statement for tax sale subsequent taxes and special assessments will be mailed to the holder of the Certificate of Purchase at Tax Sale. Taxes and special assessments for a subsequent year may be paid by the private buyer at tax sale beginning 14 days following the date from which an installment or assessment becomes delinquent. The first tax installment and special assessments become delinquent October 1 unless the last day of September is a Saturday or Sunday, and in that case, the amount due becomes delinquent the second business day of October. The second tax installment becomes delinquent April 1 unless the last day of March is a Saturday or Sunday, and in that case, the amount due becomes delinquent the second business day of April. Subsequent payments must be received in the Treasurer's Office by noon of the last business day of the month to allow adequate processing time. Otherwise, interest for the succeeding month will be collected from the tax lien holder. A postmark will not be used to calculate interest or to determine whether interest shall accrue on the subsequent payment. Any unpaid subsequent taxes and assessments will be advertised and offered at the 2008 tax sale.

8. REDEMPTION

A tax sale redemption will include the following: the original tax sale amount, including the certificate fee paid at the time of the tax sale; interest of 2 percent per month calculated against the original tax sale amount with each fraction of a month being counted as a whole month; subsequent taxes and/or special assessments paid by the tax sale purchaser and added to the amount of the sale, with interest of 2 percent per month calculated from the date of payment, with each fraction of a month being counted as a whole month; statutorily allowed costs incurred for action taken toward obtaining a tax sale deed that are recorded with the filing of the completed affidavit of service in the Treasurer's Office prior to redemption. All interest is rounded to the nearest whole dollar.

Guaranteed funds redemptions are collected by the Treasurer's Office. Upon letter notification by the Treasurer's Office of a redemption, the private buyer at tax sale must forward the original Certificate of Purchase at tax sale to the Treasurer's Office. A redemption check will then be mailed to the private buyer at tax sale.

9. PROCEEDING TO THE TAKING OF TAX SALE DEED

The Code of Iowa provides that after one year and nine months from the date of purchase at the Regular Tax Sale, nine months from the date of purchase at the Public Bidder Tax Sale, and three months from the date of purchase at the Public Nuisance Tax Sale, the holder of the Certificate of Purchase at Tax Sale may cause the service of a Notice of Expiration of Right of Redemption and Taking of Tax Sale Deed. Notice shall be served upon all parties having an interest of record in the property in the manner prescribed by law. It is strongly recommended that a buyer at tax sale retain the services of an attorney to complete this process.

After the service is completed, the certificate holder must file an affidavit with the Treasurer's Office, stating who was served, in what manner they were served and the costs involved. If the tax sale is not redeemed within 90 days from the date of the filing of the affidavit of service, a tax sale deed will be issued by the Treasurer's Office to the certificate holder. The fee for the issuance of a tax sale deed is $25. Further, the Treasurer's Office is charged with the collection of recording fees from the tax lien holder and the recording of the tax sale deed with the County Recorder prior to the delivery of the deed to the private buyer at tax sale. The tax sale certificate holder must return the original Certificate of Purchase at Tax Sale and remit the appropriate deed issuance and recording fee to the Treasurer's Office within 90 calendar days after the redemption period expires. By statute, the Treasurer's Office must cancel the certificate for any tax sale certificate holder who fails to comply. In the case of a certificate cancellation, the tax lien holder will not receive a monetary refund from the Treasurer's Office. Because recording fees vary, a tax lien holder who intends to take deed to a parcel should telephone the Treasurer's Office at (319) 833-3013 to ascertain the recording fee.

After three years have elapsed from the date of the Regular or Public Bidder Tax Sale, and one year from the date of the Public Nuisance tax sale, if action has not been completed which qualifies the holder of the certificate to obtain a tax sale deed, the Treasurer must cancel the tax sale certificate pursuant to the Code of Iowa. No moneys will be refunded by the Treasurer's Office to the tax sale certificate holder whose lien is canceled for failure to proceed to the taking of tax sale deed.

10. GENERAL INFORMATION

When a private buyer purchases at tax sale, the taxes are being purchased, not the property. The holder of the Certificate of Purchase at Tax Sale does not have use of the property until, through due process of law, a tax sale deed is issued.

If taxes or special assessments are erroneously offered for sale and sold, the bid amount will be refunded with no interest earned.

A tax sale can be set aside in a situation where a combination of bidders agrees not to compete with each other in the bid down process and one of them becomes the tax sale buyer. Such fraudulent collusion prevents selling a delinquency for the smallest percentage of undivided interest in the parcel.

Further, a Certificate of Purchase at Tax Sale or tax sale deed can be set aside if it is determined that the tax sale or assignee was ineligible to purchase the tax sale Certificate. The general rule is that a tax sale buyer or assignee should never have an interest in the parcel whose delinquencies are offered for sale. A prospective bidder should consult with legal counsel to determine the right to become a tax sale buyer, either through bid or assignment.

This document has been prepared to provide general information and guidelines relative to the tax sale, certificate assignment, redemption, and issuance of a tax sale deed. It is not an all-inclusive listing of statutory requirements, procedures, or policy. It is not to be construed as a legal opinion of the statutes governing tax sales.

KANSAS

JOHNSON COUNTY, KANSAS
Web site for information:
legal.jocogov.org/tax_sale.htm

AUCTION PROCEDURES
County tax auctions are held to collect unpaid real estate taxes. This outline will help you understand the process and the research you will need to do if you are interested in purchasing property at the tax auction.

- There may be more than one tax foreclosure in progress at any given time, and each one may be at a different stage of the process. Auctions will be set as needed throughout the year.
- Several properties may be offered for individual auction at an auction.
- The County does not sell tax lien certificates.
- **You are responsible for researching the properties that interest you** to determine whether they are suitable for your use. Some examples of research you may want to do are: determine the location and type of property; check with the city and/or County for zoning and building limitations; check with the County appraiser for assessed value and current tax rates; check with the Department of Records & Tax Administration for easements and restrictive covenants; and view the property. Additional research may be appropriate. Seek individual legal advice.
- A list of the properties, as well as the date, time, and location of the auction and registration requirements will be published prior to the auction in the *Kansas City Star* and the *Olathe Daily News* once a week for three weeks. You may also view a list of properties at the Web site.
- Also, you may obtain a list of the properties at the Johnson County Legal Department. Properties are listed by parcel

identification number and by legal description; approximate addresses are listed where available but are not warranted. You may view maps of the properties at the Web site; the maps follow the list of properties.

- Booklets containing lists and maps of the properties are also available at the Johnson County Legal Department. Booklets may be obtained in person or by mail. To order the booklet by mail, send your name and address to Johnson County Legal Department, 111 S. Cherry Street, Suite 3200, Olathe, KS 66061-3486.
- The amount of tax listed for each property in the auction notice is the amount of delinquent taxes owed, plus interest, not the assessed value.
- Ownership of the property remains with the current owner(s) until the auction. Therefore, you may not enter the property without the permission of the owner(s).
- The current owner(s) may redeem the property at any time prior to the time of auction.

THE AUCTION

- Properties are sold at public auction to the highest qualified bidder, as defined by state statute. The County may bid on properties up to the amount of taxes and interest it is owed.
- Generally, state law prohibits the following people from buying at the auction:
  a. those who owe delinquent taxes in Johnson County;
  b. those who have an interest in the property, such as the owners, relatives, or officers of a corporation which owns the property; and
  c. those who buy the property with the intent to transfer it to someone who is prohibited from buying at the auction.
- Some properties may sell for less than the taxes owed; some may sell for more.
- Registration prior to the auction is required. Registration will be held the morning of the auction, as advertised.

- All bidders and buyers must execute an affidavit, under oath, that they meet the statutory qualifications for bidding on tax auction property.
- Properties will be sold by legal description and by County parcel identification number.
- **PROPERTIES ARE SOLD "AS IS." THERE ARE NO WARRANTIES.**
- All the properties must be paid for by the stated time on the day of the auction. Only cash, a cashier's check, or a money order will be accepted. Personal checks are not accepted.
- You may leave the building to obtain the cash, money order, or certified check for payment, but you must return to pay for the property by 4:00 PM that day. Payments will be accepted until noon at the auction site. Payments will be accepted from noon to 4:00 PM at the Johnson County Sheriff's Civil Division, 125 North Cherry Street, Room 122, Olathe, Kansas.
- The buyer must pay the fee for filing the deed with the Department of Records & Tax Administration at the time of the auction.
- The buyer will receive a receipt for payment on the day of the auction.

AFTER THE AUCTION

- The court will hold a hearing approximately three weeks after the auction to determine whether to confirm the auctions.
- Some properties sold at the auction are subject to federal lien. A deed will be issued for those properties after the expiration of the applicable federal redemption period, if the federal agency chooses not to redeem the property.
- For properties not subject to a federal lien, the Sheriff will issue a Sheriff's Deed after the court confirms the auction.
- All other liens which were of record will be extinguished upon confirmation of the auction; however, covenants, and

restrictions and easements of record are not extinguished, and the buyer takes the property subject to those encumbrances.

- The buyer is responsible for any taxes and assessments, which are not included in the judgment, including the full amount of taxes assessed against the property for the calendar year in which the auction is held.

- The buyer is responsible for taking any necessary legal action to obtain possession of the property, such as by filing an eviction proceeding.

- For 12 months after the deed is recorded, a legal challenge may still be made to question the procedures that the County followed. If such a challenge is successful, the property could revert to the original owner, in which case the court would order the purchase price refunded to the buyer.

FREQUENT QUESTIONS

Q: What is the date, time, and location of your tax auctions?

A: Auctions are scheduled when all other tax auction procedures required by law and County policy have been completed. Auction dates, times, and location will be posted on the Web site as they are set.

Q: When and how are your tax auctions advertised? How can I obtain a list of properties for upcoming auctions?

A: A list of the properties, as well as the date, time and location of the auction and registration requirements will be published prior to the auction in the *Kansas City Star* and the *Olathe Daily News* once a week for three weeks. A list of the properties and maps for the properties are available for viewing on the Web site. Also, you may obtain a list of the properties and maps at the Johnson County Legal Department. Maps and lists may be obtained in person or by mail. To order the maps and lists by mail, send your name and address to Johnson County Legal Department, 111 S. Cherry Street, Suite 3200, Olathe, KS 66061-3486.

Q: What payment requirements do you have at the auction?

A: Only cash, a cashier's check, or a money order will be accepted. Personal checks will not be accepted.

Q: Is payment in full required on the day of the auction?

A: Yes. All properties must be paid for by the stated time on the day of the auction.

Q: Does Johnson County offer a financing program?

A: No.

Q: What type of ownership document is issued at the auction?

A: The buyer will receive a receipt for payment on the day of the auction. The court will hold a hearing approximately three weeks after the auction to determine whether to confirm the auctions. For properties not subject to a federal lien, the

Sheriff will issue a Sheriff's Deed after the court confirms the auction. Some properties sold at the auctions are subject to a federal lien. A Sheriff's Deed will be issued for those properties upon the expiration of the applicable federal redemption period—if the federal agency chooses not to redeem the property. If the federal agency redeems the property, no deed will be issued and the person with the winning bid at the auction will receive a refund.

Q: Once a property is acquired through a tax auction, is there a redemption period before the purchaser may take possession?

A: No, with these exceptions: Some properties are subject to federal lien. The federal agency may redeem the property during the applicable federal redemption period. A deed will not be issued by the Sheriff until expiration of the federal redemption period and only if the federal agency does not redeem the property. All properties are subject to the *Service Members Civil Relief Act.*

Q: Does Johnson County allow investors to purchase at tax auctions without attending the tax auction?

A: Yes, but the investor's agent must register prior to the auction and must attend and bid at the auction. Further, if the investor is the successful bidder, the investor must execute the required affidavit in the allotted time—generally within 48 hours after the auction. All bidders must register prior to the auction. Registration will be held the morning of the auction. The successful bidders and buyers must execute an affidavit, under oath, that they meet the statutory qualifications for bidding on tax auction property. Generally, Kansas law prohibits the following people from buying at the auction: (1) those who owe delinquent taxes in Johnson County; (2) those who have an interest in the property, for example, owners, relatives, or officers of a corporation that owns the property; and (3) those who buy the property with the intent to transfer it to someone who is prohibited from buying.

Q: What happens to properties that do not sell at the auction? May they be purchased directly from Johnson County?

A: In the event that all the properties are not sold at an auction, Johnson County will consider all available options and procedures allowed by state law for addressing the unsold properties, including offering those properties again, at the next auction. Offers to purchase properties that did not sell at public auction will be considered and may be accepted upon published notice and court approval.

Q: Do you have a mailing list?

A: No.

Q: Does Johnson County sell tax liens?

A: No. Kansas law does not provide for the auction of tax liens.

Q: Will there be a minimum bid?

A: The County may choose to bid in at an amount up to the amount of its lien, thereby setting a minimum bid. However, the County is not required to do so.

Q: Will the properties sell for the amount of taxes owed?

A: They may sell for more; they may sell for less.

Q: What types of properties are in the auctions?

A: All types. Some have buildings or houses; some are vacant; some are very small strips of land. It is the buyer's responsibility to research the property to determine whether it is suitable for the buyer.

WASHINGTON, D.C.

Web site for information:

otr.cfo.dc.gov/otr/cwp/view,a,1330,q,594443,otrNav_gid, 1679,otrNav, |33288|.asp

REAL PROPERTY TAX SALE

As required by D.C. Statute, the Office of Tax and Revenue (OTR) holds a public auction each July to sell real property tax liens—both commercial and residential—for which property taxes were unpaid during the previous tax year. Property owners have until the date of this tax sale to pay their taxes in full, including penalties and interest, to prevent their property from being auctioned.

A list of all tax sale properties, sorted by parcel, square, suffix, and lot number with the name of the owner of record and the unpaid tax amount, is advertised in local newspapers the month prior to the auction. The advertised list is also made available for download on the Web site.

Property owners wishing to settle their tax obligations prior to the tax sale should pay their outstanding tax liabilities reflected in their final bill. Anyone with questions about the status of their property should call OTR's Customer Service Center at (202) 727-4TAX (727-4829).

B

ACTION PLANS
Now Get Out There!

ACTION PLAN FOR LIEN INVESTORS

Date Completed

1. Read and study this book.   _____

2. Pick one to three counties in one or two states to work on (this could be counties that are close to you or have upcoming sales or allow sales over-the-counter).   _____

3. Speak with county officials in each county selected. Get their materials for bidding, registration, a list of liens available, etc.   _____

4. Calendar the auctions.   _____

5. Attend an auction.   _____

6. Buy a lien at an auction.   _____

7. Have your lien redeemed (i.e., get a check from the county!).   _____

8. Buy multiple liens at another auction or over-the-counter.   _____

ACTION PLAN FOR DEED INVESTORS

Date Completed

1. Read and study this book.   _____

2. Pick one to three counties in one or two states to work on (this could be counties that are close to you or have upcoming sales or allow sales over-the-counter). _____

3. Speak with county officials in each county selected. Get their materials for bidding, registration, a list of properties available, etc. _____

4. Calendar the auctions.   _____

5. Do research on selected properties (see section on doing research). These properties may be over-the-counter or for upcoming auctions. _____

6. View each property and take a picture of it if you like it. _____

7. For the properties in which you are interested, contact a local broker about a possible resale value and his or her terms of sale (i.e., commission, length of listing, advertising). _____

8. Bid on chosen properties either over-the-counter or at an auction. _____

9. Acquire a property.   _____

10. If necessary, contact a local title company or attorney to "quiet the title" (see section on foreclosure).

11. Sell the property (either with or without a broker). _____

12. Repeat the process.   _____